OBTAINING
YOUR CALLING
AND ELECTION

OBTAINING YOUR CALLING AND ELECTION

A study of the doctrines of
faith, hope, and charity.

Kevan Kingsley Clawson
and
Terri Hopkins Clawson

(signature: Kevan Clawson)

(signature: Terri Clawson)

Walking the Line Publications   South Jordan, Utah

Other books by Kevan Clawson
Psalms to the Lord
The Atonement of Jesus Christ
The Second Coming of Jesus Christ
A Life of Miracles
Becoming a Great Missionary

Cover Design: Jaime Clawson
Electronic Page Makeup: Jennifer Asplund
Editing: John E. Hopkins
Printer and Binder: Printed in the USA by Morris Publishing, 3212 E. Highway 30, Kearney,
   NE 68847, (800) 650-7888

ISBN 0-9714540-3-5

Dedicated to

Elder Hugh W. and Anne Pinnock:

*Who taught us that perfection was possible
because God overlooks our small flaws
and makes our weaknesses strengths.*

and

John and Nancy Hopkins

*Righteous parents who encourage probing
thought and teach by example.*

Contents

Introduction

The doctrine of "election" is perhaps the most intriguing mystery of our age—that a person can actually be *guaranteed* to obtain the Celestial Kingdom of God. There is an incredible amount of information available concerning this subject and yet, at the same time, very few people have even the most basic understanding of this important doctrine. Almost every book of scripture, both ancient and modern (from the Old Testament of the Prophet Moses to the modern-day Doctrine and Covenants of Joseph Smith), clearly state the specific steps one must take in order to obtain the Kingdom of God. In fact, during the last years of his life, the Prophet Joseph Smith spoke frequently and at length on the doctrine of calling and election and encouraged the saints to obtain it for themselves. As recently as the 1980s, just prior to his death, the Apostle Bruce R. McConkie spoke fervently to the saints about obtaining their calling and election.

Christians have studied the doctrines of faith, hope, and charity for thousands of years because the scriptures make it clear these doctrines are some of the most important ever revealed to man. But even though men have spent years studying and writing about these doctrines, in most instances they have simply repeated generalized platitudes in an attempt to describe the meaning of these celestial ideas without really coming to understand their true meaning or purpose.

Insight into these doctrines has remained hidden because most people have a belief system based on the tenets of "saved by grace." These popular doctrines place all of the responsibility of salvation solely upon Jesus Christ, without putting any responsibility on the individual himself. But the true meaning of faith, hope, and charity springs from an understanding that we are personally responsible for our own actions, and, as a result, we are responsible for our own salvation.

As men prepare themselves to inherit the highest degree of glory in the Celestial Kingdom of God, they move through the very specific steps laid out by the Savior. These steps include being "called" into the work of the earthly kingdom or church, being "elected" or invited to enter the heavenly kingdom, and then, after being tested and proven, to have their election to that kingdom "made sure" or "sealed" by a priesthood ordinance. The steps required for men to have their calling and election made sure follow exactly the doctrines of faith, hope, and charity.

In this book we will provide new definitions of all of these important doctrines, and show how, by looking at these doctrines in a different way, you will be able to see why they are important and how they can actually be used in your life to obtain the Celestial Kingdom of God.

A word of caution: when a person comes to understand these doctrines correctly, that person will have to take upon himself more responsibility than he has previously assumed. Sometimes ignorance *is* bliss. It should be well understood by those seeking the Kingdom of God that when a new doctrine is revealed to a person, he becomes responsible to live that doctrine. As you go through this book and learn, perhaps for the first time, the real meanings behind the doctrines of faith, hope and charity, you will be under the obligation to live them! It will become a whole new world for all who are willing to follow their beliefs with actions. It is our hope and prayer you will indeed be motivated by our words to change your life and put into action the new doctrines learned in this book.

We will begin our study of this subject by reviewing the Kingdoms of God and the various requirements that each person must meet in order to obtain the Celestial Kingdom. Then we will look at a list of people who the scriptures document obtained their election into the Kingdom of God. By understanding what the requirements are to obtain the Kingdom of God, and seeing the type of people who will be living in that kingdom, we will better understand what we must *become* in order to get there ourselves.

Once we have a vision of where we are going, we will look at the doctrines that must be learned and the specific actions that must be taken in order to get to that kingdom we have seen in the distance. Our hope is that those who read this book will take what they learn and reach a new level of understanding as well as a commitment to go forward with renewed faith and determination to achieve the Kingdom of God for themselves.

OBTAINING YOUR
CALLING AND ELECTION

Chapter One
The Kingdoms of God

THE SONS OF PERDITION / OUTER DARKNESS

When Satan rebelled against God and Christ in the premortal life, he was called "Perdition" (which means "great sorrow"), because all those living in heaven wept over the incident.[1] All of those spirits that followed Satan, and all who follow after him in this life, are called "Sons" of Perdition.

It may surprise many to learn that it is just as difficult to become a Son of Perdition as it is to become worthy to obtain the Celestial Kingdom.[2] It is important to note that when Doctrine and Covenants Section 76 was given to the Prophet Joseph, the arrangement and explanation of the Kingdoms of God were not given in order. One would assume that God would either start with the Sons of Perdition and then work up to the Celestial Kingdom in a logical order; or just the opposite, He would start at the highest Kingdom and work down. It is significant that God chose to reveal this information "out of order," so to speak. The reason for this becomes clear when one understands that those who will enter the Celestial Kingdom and those who

---

[1] D&C 76:26
[2] See Note 1

1

will be cast out with Satan and his angels come from the same group of people! Both must have been faithful members of the Church of Jesus Christ of Latter-day Saints and have had the testimony of God borne to their souls by the Holy Ghost. One group chooses to continue in the path that leads to glory, the other chooses to reject the light and fight against God to the point of committing murder. Even though both groups have the same potential (or perhaps one could say they have the same "intensity" of spirit), one group chooses to continue to follow Christ; the other chooses to follow Satan.

If a person has enough light and truth to enter the Celestial Kingdom, he has enough light and truth to become a Son of Perdition if he chooses to do so. *All faithful members of the Church are eligible to become Sons of Perdition.*

To become a Son of Perdition, one must first become a member of the Church of Jesus Christ of Latter-day Saints. After obtaining a testimony of Christ through the power of the Holy Ghost, they must turn from God, deny the truth, and defy the knowledge and power of God.[3] Finally, after regressing into works of darkness, they "deny the spirit of the Holy Ghost" within them by committing murder.[4] *Blasphemy against the Holy Ghost (the unpardonable sin) is the act of murder.*

> *The blasphemy against the Holy Ghost, which shall not be forgiven in the world nor out of the world, is in that ye commit murder wherein ye shed innocent blood, and assent unto my death, after ye have received my new and everlasting covenant, saith the Lord God; (D&C 132:27)*

Once a murder has been committed, there can be no forgiveness in this world or in the eternal worlds to come.[5] This terrible act of evil changes a person's spirit in a way that cannot be reversed or repented of. They cannot enter any Kingdom of God because they no longer have any spiritual power.[6]

---

[3] D&C 76:31–35
[4] D&C 42:18; Alma 39:5
[5] D&C 76:34
[6] D&C 29:29

Although the ultimate fate of the Sons of Perdition is unknown,[7] the scriptures do give us a glimpse into their final punishment: they will be the only ones who will suffer a second death.[8] They are the only children of God who will not eventually be saved in one of the Kingdoms of God.[9]

This concept of a second death has been misunderstood by many, and yet it is a very simple principle. All who come upon this earth will die and all will be resurrected, including the Sons of Perdition.[10] However, after being resurrected, the Sons of Perdition will be judged and sentenced to a second death—a second separation of body and spirit, a second banishment from the presence of God. Then, as spirits, they will be subject to Satan, and all the evil spirits who have ever followed Satan will suffer a final fate together.[11]

> . . . and fire came down from God out of Heaven, and devoured them. And the Devil that deceived them was cast into the lake of fire and brimstone, where the beast and the false prophet are, and shall be tormented day and night for ever and ever. (Revelation 20:9,10)

> God will make a desolation of those bodies and spirits, and he will throw them back into the earth; that is, that portion that belongs to the earth will go back there. And so it will be with our spirits: they will go back into the elements or space that they once occupied before they came here. (Heber C. Kimball, Journal of Discourses, 5:271)

Satan and all the sons of God who follow him will be destroyed by Michael the Archangel. *After* the millennium, in the last great battle on earth called "the Battle of the Great God," Michael will lead the forces of God against the forces of Satan, including all of the wicked who have been resurrected, and all of the mortals who also follow him.

---

[7] D&C 76:45–47
[8] D&C 76:37
[9] D&C 76:38
[10] 1 Corinthians 15:21–22
[11] 2 Nephi 9:8–9

This great battle will end with the destruction of all the wicked: their physical bodies will be destroyed by fire. Then, after their bodies are destroyed, Michael will cause the spirits of Satan and all those who followed him from the beginning, to be cast into a bottomless pit,[12] a black hole in the universe. They will be sent to a place where all the progression they have obtained as spirits will be reversed, and they will eventually be changed back into their original essence: an intelligence. Then, like clay in a potter's workshop, they will be reshaped to start the journey again![13] Perhaps this time they will progress with more positive results. This true doctrine is where the false teaching of reincarnation came from.

> *The first death is the separation of the spirit from the body; the second death is the dissolution of the organized particles which compose the spirit, and their return to their native element. (Brigham Young,* Journal of Discourses, *9:149)*

> *The clay that was marred in the potter's hands was thrown back into the unprepared portion, to be prepared over again. So it will be with every wicked man and woman . . . they will be thrown back to the native element from which they originated, to be worked over again, and be prepared to enjoy some sort of a kingdom. (George A. Smith,* Journal of Discourses, *2:24)*

THE TELESTIAL WORLDS

Those who enter the lowest Kingdom of God will dwell on a telestial world. They are the wicked. They never accept the Gospel of Jesus Christ.[14] They will suffer in Hell (Spirit Prison) after their physical deaths and remain in Hell from the time of their death until the time of their resurrection at the *end* of the millennium (at least 1,000 years!).[15] They are liars, adulterers, thieves, whores and whoremasters,

---

[12] Revelation 20:3
[13] See Note 2
[14] D&C 76:82
[15] D&C 76:84–85, 102, 106

4

etc.[16] They do not become Sons of Perdition because they have not accepted the Gospel and therefore do not commit the unpardonable sin.[17]

Even though this is the lowest Kingdom of God, it is beautiful beyond description.[18] Remember, this *is* a Kingdom of God; this is part of the glory of Heaven. *We now live on a telestial world.*

An inhabitant of a telestial world will become a servant to all beings of a higher order.[19] These worlds will be ruled by beings living on terrestrial worlds, or by angels assigned to them. They will be permitted to have the influence, inspiration, and blessings that come from the Holy Ghost, but will never know the presence of Jesus Christ or God the Father.[20]

THE TERRESTRIAL WORLDS

Those who will enter the middle Kingdom of God and will dwell on terrestrial worlds are people who are basically good in heart. They are good members of other churches who were blinded or deceived by false doctrines.[21] They are members of the Church of Jesus Christ of Latter-day Saints who received a testimony of Christ, but produced no fruits. They knew the truth but were unwilling to accept and/or magnify callings given them by church authorities. They were afraid to tell others about the gospel and its truths.[22] They were inactive and lukewarm.[23]

The terrestrial world also includes those who rejected the Gospel in mortality but, after suffering the buffetings of Satan in Hell (Spirit

---

[16] D&C 76:103
[17] D&C 7:83
[18] D&C 76:89
[19] D&C 76:112
[20] D&C 76:86, 88
[21] D&C 76:75
[22] Matthew 25:14–30; D&C 76:79
[23] Revelation 3:15–16

Prison) and being taught the gospel by righteous missionaries from Paradise, finally accepted the gospel. However, it is too late for them to accept the temple work done in their behalf by the righteous still living on earth.[24] (Temple ordinances are only for those who will enter the Celestial Kingdom!)

Also included in this kingdom are those who died without knowing or understanding the Gospel Law (generally speaking, the Heathen Nations of the earth).[25] Their birth and station in this life (the reason they were not in a position to hear the gospel on earth) was due to their lack of faithfulness in the premortal life. Though they, too, will eventually hear and accept the gospel, they have weak spirits, incapable of rising to a higher level.

> *Now, I wish to say to you that those who died without law, meaning the pagan nations, for lack of faithfulness, for lack of devotion, in the former life, are obtaining all that they are entitled to. I don't mean to say that all of them will be barred from entrance into the highest glory. Any one of them who repents and complies with the conditions might also obtain celestial glory, but the greatest bulk of them will only obtain terrestrial glory. (Sermons of Melvin Ballard, 1949, p. 246)*

Though the conditions and glory of the terrestrial world will exceed in every way those of the telestial world, they too become servants to all beings of a higher order.[26] Terrestrial worlds will be ruled by those of a celestial glory and will receive the blessing of being visited from time to time by Jesus Christ[27] but are denied the presence of the Father. During the millennium, the earth will be changed from its telestial order to the higher, terrestrial order.

---

[24] D&C 76:73–74
[25] D&C 76:72
[26] D&C 76:91
[27] D&C 76:77, 87

THE CELESTIAL WORLDS

All who enter the Celestial Kingdom will have to have their calling and election made sure and be sealed to eternal life *before* entering their Kingdom of Glory. This statement may surprise some, but the requirements for this kingdom are the same for everyone and do not change—whether in mortal life or in the spirit world or in the eternal worlds to come. It is possible to be sealed in this mortal life and know ahead of time that you will enter the Celestial Kingdom. But whether in this life or the next, a person must officially enter the Church of the Firstborn through a priesthood ordinance, and this ordinance must be performed *prior* to a person entering the Celestial Kingdom.

In order for anyone to enter the Celestial Kingdom, they must follow the same path the Savior did:

> *They must receive a testimony of Jesus Christ.[28]*
> *They must be baptized by one having authority.[29]*
> *They must receive the Holy Ghost by the laying on of hands.[30]*
> *Then must accept and magnify callings in the church,[31] and the men must be ordained to the Melchizedek Priesthood.[32]*
> *By the strength of their faith, they overcome Satan's temptations, and endure to the end.[33]*
> *Finally, they are sealed by the "Holy Spirit of Promise," which accepts and ratifies all of their works and the righteous acts they have done.[34]*

> *The Holy Spirit of Promise is the Holy Ghost who places the stamp of approval upon every ordinance that is done righteously and when covenants are broken he removes the seal.*
> *(Joseph Fielding Smith,* Doctrines of Salvation *1:55)*

---

[28] D&C 76:51
[29] D&C 76:51
[30] D&C 76:52
[31] D&C 76:79
[32] D&C 84:33–41
[33] D&C 76:53
[34] D&C 76:53

When all of these steps have been taken, a specific priesthood ordinance must be performed that formally seals the person into the Celestial Kingdom. This ordinance is known as the "more sure word of prophecy."

> The more sure word of prophecy means a man's knowing that he is sealed up unto eternal life, by revelation and the spirit of prophecy, through the power of the Holy Priesthood. (D&C 131:5)

Joseph Smith goes on to state: "It is impossible for a man to be saved in ignorance."[35] This does not mean that "knowledge" is a requirement for entering the Celestial Kingdom. (Remember, little children who die go to the Celestial Kingdom, even though they have no "knowledge"; also, think of the many pioneers who died crossing the plains—many of whom could not read or write and had never read the scriptures. Surely they would not be denied entrance into the kingdom because they were "ignorant.") This statement refers to the doctrine of being sealed to eternal life. Since all people who enter the Celestial Kingdom must first be sealed by a priesthood ordinance, everyone will know ahead of time whether they will enter the kingdom; therefore, no one will be surprised by their reward, or saved in ignorance.

When taken in full context, the revelation to Joseph Smith becomes clear (read D&C 131:5–6 together; you will note that in the introduction to this section, those verses were written to be read as one thought!).

THE LOWEST DEGREE OF THE CELESTIAL KINGDOM

This level of celestial glory is provided for righteous people who do not have the natural intelligence or ability to become like God. They will not be rulers of worlds, but will become servants.

---

[35] D&C 131:6

Those who receive a lesser degree in the celestial kingdom, will not be made equal in power, might, and dominion, and many blessings of the exaltation will be denied them. We learn from the Book of Abraham that some intelligences are greater than others and so will it be in the celestial kingdom. (Joseph Fielding Smith, Church History and Modern Revelation, *2:57,58)*

THE MIDDLE DEGREE OF THE CELESTIAL KINGDOM

This level of celestial glory is provided for righteous people who have the natural ability to become like God but have chosen not to marry. They too will become servants, living singly and separately forever.[36]

Will there be any difference among those who are redeemed into that celestial glory? There will. They will all be equal in the enjoyment of some blessings, and their glory will be the same, but yet in some respects there will be a difference. Some who will inherit a portion of that glory will have no families, they will be deprived of that blessing to all ages of eternity, while others will receive an exaltation and kingdom, and will have wives, children, dominion, greatness and power far above those I first referred to. Now why should there be this distinction in the celestial kingdom, and what is the cause of it? It is because certain persons who have obeyed the Gospel have become careless and indifferent in regard to securing that high exaltation which was within their reach. (Orson Pratt, Journal of Discourses, *15:319)*

THE HIGHEST DEGREE OF THE CELESTIAL KINGDOM

This level of celestial glory can only be obtained by entering into the new and everlasting covenant of eternal marriage. The last ordinance a man or woman completes to prepare themselves to obtain

---

[36] D&C 132:16–17

their Calling and Election to the Kingdom of God is to be sealed for eternity to a spouse of their choosing in a temple of God.

> *In the celestial glory there are three heavens or degrees; And in order to obtain the highest, a man must enter into this order of the priesthood (meaning the new and everlasting covenant of marriage); And if he does not, he cannot obtain it. He may enter into the other, but that is the end of his kingdom; he cannot have an increase. (D&C 131:1–4)*

It is made clear through modern day revelation that in heaven men and women live as family units. Most Christian religions teach "until death do you part," that once dead, men and women live singly and separately as angels in heaven, servants to God. But we are fortunate to have the truth revealed in our day: that God himself is married, that we have a mother in heaven, and that we are literally children of God! To become like God, we too must be married and create a family unit of our own.

> *Implicit in the Christian verity that all men are the spirit children of an Eternal Father is the usually unspoken truth that they are also the offspring of an Eternal Mother. An exalted and glorified Man of Holiness (Moses 6:57) could not be a Father unless a Woman of like glory, perfection, and holiness was associated with him as a Mother. This begetting of children makes a man a father and a woman a mother whether we are dealing with man in his mortal or immortal state.*

> *This doctrine that there is a Mother in Heaven was affirmed in plainness by the First Presidency of the Church (Joseph F. Smith, John R. Winder, and Anthon H. Lund) when, in speaking of pre-existence and the origin of man, they said that "man, as a spirit, was begotten and born of heavenly parents, and reared to maturity in the eternal mansions of the Father," that man is the "offspring of celestial parentage," and that "all men and women are in the similitude of the universal Father and Mother and are literally the sons and daughters of Deity." (*Man: Origin and Destiny, *pp. 248–355).*

10

This glorious truth of celestial parentage, including specifically both a Father and a Mother, is heralded forth by song in one of the greatest of Latter-day Saint hymns. O My Father by Eliza R. Snow, written in 1843, during the lifetime of the Prophet, includes this teaching:

> In the heavens are parents single? No; the thought makes reason stare! Truth is reason, truth eternal, Tells me I've a Mother there.
>
> When I leave this frail existence, When I lay this mortal by, Father, Mother, may I meet you in your royal courts on high?
>
> Then, at length, when I've completed All you sent me forth to do, With your mutual approbation, Let me come and dwell with you.

*Mortal persons who overcome all things and gain an ultimate exaltation will live eternally in the family unit and have spirit children, thus becoming Eternal Fathers and Eternal Mothers (D&C 132:19–32). Indeed, the formal pronouncement of the Church, issued by the First Presidency and the Council of the Twelve, states: "So far as the stages of eternal progression and attainment have been made known through divine revelation, we are to understand that only resurrected and glorified beings can become parents of spirit offspring. (*Man: His Origin and Destiny, p. 129)" (Bruce R. McConkie, *Mormon Doctrine, pp. 517–517 "Mother in Heaven")*

All those who expect to enter the highest degree of the Celestial Kingdom must be married. In the eternities to come, our kingdom, the place we will live and the people we will rule, will be our own creation. Living as Kings and Queens on a world we have created, our subjects will be our own children!

Who will be the subjects in the kingdom which they will rule who are exalted in the celestial kingdom of our God? Will they reign over their neighbors' children? Their own children, their own posterity will be the citizens of their kingdoms; in other words, the patriarchal order will prevail there to the endless ages of eternity, and the children of each patriarch will be his while eternal ages roll on. (Orson Pratt, Journal of Discourses, 15:319)

After obtaining the seal of eternal life, those who enter the Celestial Kingdom will have their names written in the Lamb's Book of Life. They will join the company of angels and the General Assembly and will become members of the Church of the Firstborn.[37] They become Kings and Priests, Queens and Priestesses, and inherit all that God has.[38] They not only dwell with God and Christ forever but will become Gods themselves.[39]

The importance of fulfilling each and every step on the path of salvation cannot be emphasized enough! Though we have a kind and loving Father in Heaven, a Father that desires each and every one of his spirit children to return to His presence, God is bound by the covenants we make with him and the eternal laws that govern our existence. We cannot enter the highest degree of the Celestial Kingdom unless we fulfill each and every step required for entrance.

> *For behold, I reveal unto you a new and an everlasting covenant; and if ye abide not that covenant, then are ye damned; for no one can reject this covenant and be permitted to enter into my glory.*

> *For all who will have a blessing at my hands shall abide the law which was appointed for that blessing, and the conditions thereof, as were instituted from before the foundation of the world.*

> *And as pertaining to the new and everlasting covenant, it was instituted for the fullness of my glory; and he that receiveth a fullness thereof must and shall abide the law, or he shall be damned, saith the Lord God.*

---

[37] D&C 76:54, 63
[38] D&C 76:55–56, 59
[39] D&C 76:58, 62; 132:17

*And verily I say unto you, that the conditions of this law are
these: All covenants, contracts, bonds, obligations, oaths,
vows, performances, connections, associations, or expecta-
tions, that are not made and entered into and sealed by the
Holy Spirit of promise, of him who is anointed, both as well
for time and for all eternity, and that too most holy, by revelation and commandment through the medium of mine
anointed, whom I have appointed on the earth to hold this
power (and I have appointed unto my servant Joseph Smith to
hold this power in the last days, and there is never but one on
the earth at a time on whom this power and the keys of this
priesthood are conferred), are of no efficacy, virtue, or force in
and after the resurrection from the dead; for all contracts that
are not made unto this end have an end when men are dead.
(D&C 132:4–7)*

Everyone who expects to obtain the Celestial Kingdom must go
through all of these steps, do so faithfully, and endure to the end.
Those who desire to obtain this seal while still in this mortal life
must not only accomplish all of these steps, but must prove themselves
in all things, even if it means the sacrifice of all their material things—
or even their own life—in the effort. The reason they must be tested
or proven to such a great extent is because God must see if they will
"endure to the end" before they actually do. In order to receive their
seal prior to death, they must pass an ultimate test of their faith, as a
sign of their spiritual strength and faithfulness (like Abraham's willingness to sacrifice his son Isaac). Those who do pass this ultimate test of
their faith are assured of receiving a place in the Celestial Kingdom.

Think of this sacrifice or test as if you were required to climb
Mount Everest in order to get to heaven. You could *prove* that you had
the ability to climb Mount Everest without actually doing it by climb-
ing other mountains that were just as difficult, or even more difficult
than your actual quest. This is what our ultimate test is like! We are
tested in a way that will prove we have the ability to endure to the end,
before we actually do. And by passing this test, we prove both to ourselves and to God that we are worthy to enter the Celestial Kingdom.

NOTES

1. Brigham Young, *Journal of Discourses*, 3:93.

"How much does it take to prepare a man, or woman, or any being to become angels to the Devil, to suffer with him to all eternity? Just as much as it does to prepare a man to go into the celestial kingdom, into the presence of the Father and the Son, and to be made an heir to his Kingdom, and all his glory, and be crowned with crowns of glory, immortality, and eternal lives."

2. D. H. Wells, *Journal of Discourses*, 5:42.

"We have the privilege of honoring the stations we are in; we have the privilege, in the Lord's hands, of preparing for exaltation. We are compared to the making of pottery upon the wheel . . . The Lord says, "You, intelligent Israel, are to blame, if you do not obey my voice; and if you are disobedient, I will serve you as the potter serves the clay . . . Consequently, the intelligence that you are endowed with will be taken from you, and you will have to go into the mill and be ground over again."

Chapter Two
Examples of Righteousness

ADAM AND EVE

Our first example of people who were sealed to eternal life while still in mortality is Adam and Eve. Although they transgressed and caused the downfall of all mankind, they repented of their mortal sins and obtained their calling and election. We can assume this to be true because they were permitted to see Jesus Christ while still in the flesh. (Seeing Christ does not necessarily mean that a person has their calling and election, but it is a strong indication.) We also know that Adam was faithful to the end and did become a God. He remains the exalted head of the human family, and it will be Adam who gives back to Christ the authority to return and rule the earth during the millennium.[1]

> *And the Lord appeared unto them, and they rose up and blessed Adam, and called him Michael, the prince, the archangel. And the Lord administered comfort unto Adam, and said unto him: I have set thee to be at the head; a multitude of nations shall come of thee, and thou art a prince over them forever. (D&C 107:54–55)*

---

[1] Daniel 7:9–10

15

In reviewing the scriptures, it becomes clear that Adam and Eve received their calling and election because of their steady faithfulness, and because they diligently taught their children the truths of the gospel.[2] Although they transgressed and fell, Adam and Eve fully repented of their mortal sins, proved their faithfulness, and were rewarded by receiving the promise of eternal life.[3]

ENOCH

Enoch received his calling and election because of his love for the Lord and his missionary work. He was called in his youth to preach repentance to the wicked people of his time, which would be a hard test for anyone. In addition, Enoch had a speech impediment and had been ridiculed and hated for it. Nonetheless, Enoch was faithful to this calling and responsibility and preached for many hundreds of years.

In time, Enoch's faith grew to the point that men trembled before him as he spoke and mountains moved from his path with only a word from his mouth.[4] Enoch was permitted to speak with the Lord face to face and saw visions of future times and places.[5] Over a long period of time, Enoch was successful in his missionary work and thousands were converted and baptized. Due to the wickedness of the world and the destruction destined to come upon the earth (the great flood), all the righteous were gathered together into one great city called Zion.[6] Just prior to the flood, Enoch and the whole city of Zion were translated, taken up into heaven to remain in a terrestrial state until the time of the Millennium.[7]

> And I saw the Lord; and he stood before my face, and he talked with me, even as a man talketh one with another, face to face; (Moses 7:4)

---

[2] Moses 5:3–16
[3] Moses 6:64–68
[4] Moses 6:47; 7:13
[5] Moses 7:4
[6] Moses 7:18–19
[7] Moses 7:21, 60–65

16

And it came to pass that the Lord showed unto Enoch all the inhabitants of the earth; and he beheld, and lo, Zion, in the process of time, was taken up into heaven. And the Lord said unto Enoch: behold mine abode forever. (Moses 7:21)

ABRAHAM

Abraham received his calling and election because of his willingness to sacrifice all things for God. He began by leaving his extended family, his land, and most of his material property to follow a promise that the Lord would lead him to a new and promised land.[8] This took incredible faith for this simple shepherd. But his faithfulness did not end there. He became a missionary, converting other members of his family and persuading them to join him in this dangerous and unpopular adventure.[9] Nor did Abraham forsake his God in trial: even after giving up so much, the Lord had not yet answered his prayers and blessed him with a son. Yet Abraham believed God's promise that he would some day have a son.[10]

Abraham, like all men, was required to make covenants with the Lord. As he progressed in faith and works, the Lord did make covenants with Abraham, and Abraham received a new name as part of that covenant. Abraham was faithful and perfect in living up to each and every covenant made with God.[11]

After entering into the initial covenants with God, Abraham was required to live the law of celestial marriage, or polygamy. The Lord asked Abraham to live this law because he knew that Abraham would teach his family the ways of God and ensure that they all kept the commandments of the Lord.[12] After proving his faithfulness in all these areas, Abraham was finally blessed with the miracle of a son.[13]

---

[8] Genesis 12:1–4
[9] Genesis 12:5
[10] Genesis 15:6
[11] Genesis 17:1–8
[12] Genesis 18:19
[13] Genesis 21:1–4

However, there was one more test of faithfulness the Lord had for Abraham; the Lord would require the sacrifice of his most cherished possession—his favorite son, Isaac. When Abraham proved his faith by fulfilling this great test, he received his calling and election and is now ruling as a God in the heavens.[14]

> *Abraham received all things, whatsoever he received, by revelation and commandment, by my word, saith the Lord, and hath entered into his exaltation and sitteth upon his throne. (D&C 132:29)*

Abraham was a wonderful example of a righteous man. He lived a perfect life and time and again proved his faithfulness by sacrificing his most precious possessions to the Lord. In addition, he became a great missionary and brought many souls unto the Lord.[15]

ISAAC

Isaac received his calling and election because of his willingness to lay down his life when asked by the Lord. Remember that Isaac was over thirty years old when Abraham was asked to sacrifice him to the Lord. Isaac could easily have overpowered his father or run for fear of his life. But Isaac's faith was the same as his father Abraham's, and Isaac willingly submitted to the test.[16]

> *And Abraham again said unto Isaac his son, Is there in thy heart any thought or counsel concerning this, which is not proper? tell me my son I pray thee, O my son conceal it not from me. And Isaac answered his father Abraham and said unto him, O my father, as the Lord liveth and as thy soul liveth, there is nothing in my heart to cause me to deviate either to the right or to the left from the word that he has spoken to thee. (The Book of Jasher 23:53–54)*

---

[14] Genesis 22:1–14
[15] See Note 1
[16] See Note 2

18

After proving his faithfulness to the Lord, Isaac received the same blessings his father Abraham had received.[17] And, like his father, Isaac was permitted to see the Lord face to face.[18]

JOB

Job received his calling and election because he lived a righteous life and, like Abraham, was tested to prove his faithfulness to God. Job is well known for the trials he endured but most forget the great blessings he received because of his righteous life.

Job was considered perfect in his day, a man who followed God with exactness and always resisted temptation.[19] God himself was impressed with the faith and spiritual strength of Job.[20] After being tested with the loss of his family, his wealth, and even his health, Job received the witness of the spirit that he would see and live with his Savior.

> For I know that my redeemer liveth, and that he shall stand at the latter day upon the earth: and though after my skin worms destroy this body, yet in my flesh shall I see God: whom I shall see for myself, and mine eyes shall behold, and not another; though my reins be consumed within me. (Job 19:25–27)

After a period of time, Job did see the Lord with his own eyes[21] and was blessed with more wealth and posterity than he had in the beginning.[22]

---

[17] Genesis 26:1–5
[18] Genesis 26:2; see Note 3
[19] Job 1:1–2
[20] Job 2:3
[21] Job 42:4–5
[22] Job 42:12–17

ENOS

Enos received his calling and election because of the pure desires of his heart to know God, and his great love for both the Nephites and the wicked Lamanites. Though it is not recorded whether Enos ever actually saw the Lord, it is clear that he was to be sealed to eternal life.

Enos was a righteous man who struggled to know God and to be forgiven of his sins.[23] After a long and difficult process of prayer and supplication, Enos was cleansed and forgiven.[24] After receiving the knowledge that his own sins were forgiven, he immediately felt a desire to save others. This began a long period of missionary work. Enos's service to the Lord began with his brethren the Nephites and over time was expanded to include the Lamanites.[25] In the end, Enos knew that he would receive eternal life and see the face of his Savior.

> And soon I go to the place of my rest, which is with my Redeemer; for I know that in him I shall rest. And I rejoice in the day when my mortal shall put on immortality, and shall stand before him; then shall I see his face with pleasure, and he will say unto me: Come unto me, ye blessed, there is a place prepared for you in the mansions of my Father. Amen. (Enos 1:27)

ALMA (THE ELDER)

Alma received his calling and election because of his faith in a Prophet of God and his priesthood service in building up the Church of Jesus Christ in his day. Alma was not a righteous man in the beginning. He was one of the wicked priests of the most notorious king in the Book of Mormon: King Noah.[26] Alma listened to the Prophet Abinadi and was converted.[27] Then Alma fled from the King and while in

---

[23] Enos 1:1–3
[24] Enos 1:4–5
[25] Enos 1:9–11, 20
[26] Mosiah 11:5–7
[27] Mosiah 16:2

hiding, recorded all of the words and teachings of the Prophet Abinadi.[28] Once truly converted, Alma began to preach the word of God secretly and obtained a small following of people.[29] Soon Alma felt the promptings of the Spirit to begin to baptize those who had followed him and organized "The Church of Christ." After many years, and even more trials, Alma and his group of followers fled to Zarahemla. Once there, Alma was authorized by King Mosiah to organize the church in all the land.[30] Finally toward the end of his life, the voice of the Lord came to Alma and promised him eternal life.

> *And blessed art thou because thou hast established a church among this people; and they shall be established, and they shall be my people. Thou art my servant; and I covenant with thee that thou shalt have eternal life. (Mosiah 26:17, 20)*

THE TWELVE APOSTLES

Christ's ancient apostles, the twelve special witnesses of his name, received their callings and elections because they were willing to give up all their worldly goods and become lifelong missionaries and servants of God.[31] Peter, as was his nature, was forward enough to ask the Lord what he would receive for following Jesus. The Lord promised eternal life to him, all the Apostles, and indeed, to all believers who do the same.

> *Then Peter began to say unto him, Lord, we have left all, and have followed thee. And Jesus answered and said, Verily I say unto you, There is no man that hath left house, or brethren, or sisters, or father, or mother, or wife, or children, or lands, for my sake, and the gospel's, but he shall receive an hundredfold now in this time, houses, and brethren, and sisters, and mothers, and children, and lands; and in the world to come eternal life. (Mark 10:28–30)*

---

[28] Mosiah 17:4
[29] Mosiah 18:1–4
[30] Mosiah 25:19–22
[31] Mark 10:28

21

THE TWELVE NEPHITE DISCIPLES

The Twelve Disciples in America received their callings and elections in an unusual way: they asked for it! After being called and set apart for service in the Kingdom of God, and knowing within themselves that they would be faithful to the end, the disciples requested a blessing of the Lord before he left them: they asked—and received—the promise of eternal life.

> *What is it that ye desire of me, after that I am gone to the Father? And they all spake, save it were three, saying: We desire that after we have lived unto the age of man, that we may speedily come unto thee in thy kingdom. And he said unto them: Blessed are ye because ye desired this thing of me; therefore, after that ye are seventy and two years old ye shall come unto me in my kingdom; and with me ye shall find rest. And he turned himself unto the three . . . and he said unto them: Behold, I know your thoughts . . . therefore, more blessed are ye, for ye shall never taste of death; but ye shall live to behold all the doings of the Father unto the children of men . . . for ye have desired that ye might bring the souls of men unto me, while the world shall stand. And for this cause ye shall have fullness of joy; and ye shall sit down in the kingdom of my Father. (3 Nephi 28:1-10)*

MORONI

Moroni received his calling and election because of his righteousness, and due to his faithfulness in keeping and protecting the sacred records of his fathers. Moroni was to see the utter destruction of all the Nephites and was left alone to wander the earth. Sometime in the loneliness and isolation of his sojourn on earth, Moroni received the promise of eternal life.

> *And it came to pass that the Lord said unto me: If they have not charity it mattereth not unto thee, thou hast been faithful; wherefore, thy garments shall be made clean. And because thou hast seen thy weakness thou shalt be made strong, even*

*unto the sitting down in the place which I have prepared in
the mansions of my Father.
(Ether 12:37)*

JOSEPH SMITH

Though Joseph Smith saw God the Father and Jesus Christ in his
youth, it was not until much later in his life that he received his calling
and election.[32] Joseph made many mistakes in his life and was punished and chastened by the Lord to learn obedience, as are all of God's
children.[33] Like the ancient apostles and prophets, Joseph gave up
most of his material wealth and a normal family life in order to serve
the Lord. His sacrifice and suffering are well documented in Church
history and in the minds and hearts of all Latter-day Saints. At some
time during his life, he too received the promise of eternal life. He
then spent a great deal of time and effort to teach the Saints this doctrine and sealed many to eternal life by his own hands.

> *For I am the Lord thy God, and will be with thee even unto the
> end of the world, and through all eternity; for verily I seal
> upon you your exaltation, and prepare a throne for you in the
> kingdom of my Father, with Abraham your Father. Behold, I
> have seen your sacrifices, and will forgive all your sins; I have
> seen your sacrifices in obedience to that which I have told you.
> Go, therefore, and I make a way for your escape, as I accepted
> the offering of Abraham of his son Isaac. (D&C 132:49–50)*

THE UNITED ORDER

When Joseph Smith introduced the doctrine of consecration, he
taught that for a person to obtain eternal life he must be willing to sacrifice all earthly possessions. In this way a person can prove to himself
and to God that he will follow God at all costs. When first attempting

---

[32] Joseph Smith History 1:17
[33] D&C Section 3

to build the city of New Jerusalem or Zion, those who participated in this great event were required to live the doctrine and Law of Consecration. Joseph began what was called "the United Order," a society where all who participated were under covenant to live the law of consecration.[34] Those who joined the United Order were required to give all of their worldly possessions to the church. In return, they were promised eternal life if they remained faithful until the end.[35] Unfortunately, this great experiment failed due to the greed and wickedness of some of those who participated. However, those who did remain faithful did receive their calling and election and the promise of eternal life.

> *Verily, thus saith the Lord unto you who have assembled yourselves together to receive his will concerning you: behold, this is pleasing unto your Lord, and the angels rejoice over you; the alms of your prayers have come up into the ears of the Lord of Sabaoth, and are recorded in the book of the names of the sanctified, even them of the celestial world. Wherefore, I now send upon you another Comforter, even upon you my friends, that it may abide in your hearts, even the Holy Spirit of promise; which other Comforter is the same that I promised unto my disciples, as is recorded in the testimony of John. This comforter is the promise which I give unto you of eternal life, even the glory of the celestial kingdom; which glory is that of the church of the Firstborn, even of God, the holiest of all, through Jesus Christ his Son. (D&C 88:1–5)*

WILLIAM CLAYTON

William Clayton was the clerk for the Church under both Joseph Smith and Brigham Young. In return for his quiet and faithful service to the Church and Joseph Smith, he received the promise of eternal life:

---

[34] D&C 78:11–12
[35] D&C 78:17–22

Your life is hid with Christ in God, and so are many others.
Nothing but the unpardonable sin [murder] can prevent you
from inheriting eternal life for you are sealed up by the power
of the Priesthood unto eternal life, having taken the step neces-
sary for that purpose. (History of the Church 5:391)

HEBER AND VILATE KIMBALL

Even before the revelation concerning celestial marriage and the
doctrine of polygamy was written down, it was shared with Heber C.
Kimball by Joseph Smith. Joseph told him that those who were asked
to practice this law must be prepared to obey it fully. But before Joseph asked Heber to enter into this sacred covenant, he tested his
faithfulness.

> *Before he would trust even Heber with the full secret, how-*
> *ever, he put him to a test which few men would have been able*
> *to bear. It was no less than a requirement for him to surrender*
> *his wife, his beloved Vilate, and give her to Joseph in mar-*
> *riage! The astounding revelation well-nigh paralyzed him. He*
> *could hardly believe he had heard aright. Yet Joseph was sol-*
> *emnly in earnest. Three days he fasted and wept and prayed.*
> *Then, with a broken and a bleeding heart, but with soul self-*
> *mastered for the sacrifice, he led his darling wife to the*
> *Prophet's house and presented her to Joseph. It was enough —*
> *the heavens accepted the sacrifice. The will for the deed was*
> *taken, and 'accounted unto him for righteousness.' Joseph*
> *wept at this proof of devotion, and embracing Heber, told him*
> *that was all that the Lord required. He had proved him, as a*
> *child of Abraham, that he would 'do the works of Abraham,'*
> *holding back nothing, but laying all upon the altar for God's*
> *glory. The Prophet joined the hands of the heroic and devoted*
> *pair, and then and there, by virtue of the sealing power and*
> *authority of the Holy Priesthood, Heber and Vilate Kimball*
> *were made husband and wife for all eternity.* (The Life of
> Heber C. Kimball, *p. 323*)

Heber's test was now over, but Vilate Kimball was to be tested yet
again by the doctrine of plural marriage. Now Heber loved Vilate

25

dearly, and it took a great deal of fasting and prayer before he could even approach Vilate to ask her to join him in accepting to live this divine practice. Vilate, knowing that something was wrong with her beloved husband, secretly prayed to the Lord to find out what the problem was. While kneeling in prayer, the Lord revealed to Vilate a vision of the Celestial Kingdom and an understanding of the doctrine and law of plural marriage. She immediately went to Heber, told him of the revelation she had received, and told him she was willing to obey.

> While pleading as one would plea for life, the vision of her mind was opened, and, as darkness flees before the morning sun, so did her sorrow vanish away. Before her was illustrated the order of celestial marriage, in all its beauty and glory, together with the great exaltation and honor it would confer upon her in that immortal and celestial sphere, if she would accept it and stand in her place by her husband's side. She also saw the vast and boundless love and union which this order would bring about, as well as the increase of her husband's kingdoms, and the power and glory extending throughout the eternities, worlds without end. (The Life of Heber C. Kimball p. 327)

Because of their faithfulness, Joseph sealed both Heber and Vilate to eternal life:

> Verily I say unto my servant Heber, thou art my son, in whom I am well pleased, for thou art careful to hearken to the words of mine anointed, even from the least to the greatest of them; therefore thy name is written in heaven, no more to be blotted out forever, because of these things. (The Life of Heber C Kimball p. 241)

> Beloved sister: I lay my hands upon your head in the name of Jesus, and seal you unto eternal life — sealed here on earth and sealed in heaven, and your name written in the Lamb's Book of Life never to be blotted out. (Principles of Power, Andrus, p. 351)

CONCLUSION

We can learn much about the process of obtaining our calling and election or being sealed to eternal life from these examples. We learn that it is not necessary to have seen Jesus Christ in order to earn this blessing (Enos and Alma). In addition, we can see that seeing Jesus Christ does not guarantee a person this blessing (Joseph Smith). We also learn that the only way to fall from this great blessing is to commit the unpardonable sin of murder (William Clayton). We learn that even though men sin, they can repent and receive forgiveness (Enos, Alma, Joseph Smith). The three things that seem to be consistent through all these examples are (1) their willingness to sacrifice, (2) their faithfulness in serving God, and (3) their ability to endure to the end of their mortal lives.

As we now look in depth at this doctrine, perhaps the most important thing we should learn from these experiences is that although living a righteous life is an important part of the process, a person can suffer weaknesses and sins and still receive the promise of eternal life. Thus, we see that every member of the Church is capable of receiving the promise of eternal life.

NOTES

1. *The Book of Jasher*, 56:11–13.
   "And Abraham planted a large grove in Beersheba, and he made to it four gates facing the four sides of the earth, and he planted a vineyard in it, so that if a traveler came to Abraham he entered any gate which was in his road, and remained there and ate and drank and satisfied himself and then departed. For the House of Abraham was always open to the sons of men that passed and repassed, who came daily to eat and drink in the house of Abraham. And any man who had hunger and came to Abraham's house, Abraham would give him bread that he might eat and drink and be satisfied, and any one that came naked to his house he would clothe with garments as he might choose, and give him silver and gold and then make known to him the Lord who had created him in the earth; this did Abraham all his life."

2. *The Book of Jasher*, 22:41–45, 53–54.
   "And when Isaac was thirty seven years old . . . Isaac answered Ishmael, saying . . . As the Lord liveth, the God of my father Abraham, if the Lord should say unto my father, take now thy son Isaac and bring him up an offering before me, I would not refrain but I would joyfully accede to it. And the Lord heard the word that Isaac spoke to Ishmael, and it seemed good in the sight of the Lord, and he thought to try Abraham in this matter.

3. *The Book of Jasher*, 23:44–45.
   "And Isaac answered and said unto his father, I see and lo a pillar of fire and a cloud, and the glory of the Lord is seen upon the cloud. And Abraham knew that his son Isaac was accepted before the Lord for a burnt offering."

Chapter Three
Terminology

Prior to beginning our discussion of the actual doctrines of faith, hope, charity, and election, it will be important to define some of these concepts in terms everyone will understand. Part of the problem people seem to have understanding these doctrines is that many of the terms are misused, interchanged, and misunderstood. The doctrines of calling, election, more sure word of prophecy, and second comforter are all distinct and separate doctrines directly related to faith, hope, and charity. Each relates to specific events and covenants that will take place in the lives of all who will see the face of God and live. In order to progress in our understanding of these doctrines, it is appropriate to define the terms we will use in our discussion. In addition, we will discuss and cast aside several misconceptions regarding this doctrine that tend to confuse and lead astray.

Calling: *Membership in the Church of Jesus Christ.*
All members of the Church, after being baptized and confirmed, are then "called" or invited to enter the Church of the Firstborn.

> *To be called is to be a member of the Church and kingdom of God on earth; it is to be numbered with the saints; it is to accept the gospel and receive the everlasting covenant . . .*
> *(Bruce R. McConkie,* Doctrinal New Testament Commentary, *3:327)*

Election: *A testimony or assurance of one's personal worthiness.*

This is a revelation from God concerning a person's standing before God: that the life they are currently leading is acceptable to God. It is a personal revelation to one's soul, by the power of the Holy Ghost, that we are leading a life that is pleasing to our Father in Heaven. It is a spiritual affirmation that if we continue to live as we are now, we will be worthy and prepared to enter the Celestial Kingdom.

Once we have changed our lives (through the process of repentance) to the point we are worthy to enter the Celestial Kingdom, we are then "elected" to enter the Church of the Firstborn.

It is important to understand that even after obtaining your calling and election a person is not *guaranteed* a place in the Celestial Kingdom. They still must endure in faithfulness to the end. It is only after making our calling and election "sure" that we receive an *unconditional* guarantee.

Made Sure/More Sure Word: *A priesthood ordinance.*

The term "calling and election *made sure*" is the final step in becoming a member of the Church of the Firstborn. The terms "made sure" or "more sure word" or "sealed" refer to a priesthood ordinance, usually performed in a temple of God by the prophet of God, that confirms a person's place in the Celestial Kingdom.

Second Comforter: *A gift of promise; Jesus Christ.*

The second comforter is the gift given to new members of the Church of the Firstborn (like the Holy Ghost is given to new members of the earthly church). The second comforter is Jesus Christ.

Church of the Firstborn: *Members of the Celestial Kingdom.*

All people who are sealed to eternal life and enter the Celestial Kingdom become members of the Church of the Firstborn.

All people must take specific steps in order to become members of the earthly Church of Jesus Christ: 1) we were *taught* the gospel, 2) we gained a *testimony* of the truth, then 3) we receive the *ordinance* of baptism by one having authority, and finally, 4) we were officially confirmed members of the Church. As a reward for the covenants we take upon ourselves, God gives us the *gift* of the first comforter: the Holy Ghost.

In the same way, there are specific steps we must take in order to become members of the Church of the Firstborn (those worthy to enter the Celestial Kingdom): 1) We must be *taught* about celestial doctrines and covenants, 2) we must gain a personal *testimony* of our worthiness to enter the Celestial Kingdom, 3) we must have a *priesthood ordinance* performed by one having authority, and finally, 4) we will be officially confirmed members of the Church of the Firstborn. As a reward for taking upon us these higher covenants, God gives us the *gift* of the second comforter.

> *Those members of the Church who devote themselves wholly to righteousness, living by every word that proceedeth forth from the mouth of God, make their calling and election sure. That is, they receive the more sure word of prophecy, which means that the Lord seals their exaltation upon them while they are yet in this life.* (Bruce R. McConkie, **Mormon Doctrine**, *p. 109*)

These concepts will become clearer as we look at each step—in the process from first hearing the gospel and gaining faith to receiving the ultimate blessing of being sealed to eternal life by one having authority.

MISCONCEPTIONS

There are a number of misconceptions concerning what obtaining one's calling and election means, and how one actually obtains this great blessing. Unfortunately, these misconceptions prevent many people from seriously seeking—and eventually obtaining—their calling and election. The following are some of the more prevalent and damaging of these false teachings.

1. *Many have been taught that a person must have a personal visit from Jesus Christ to obtain this blessing.* But this is not true. *You do not have to see Jesus Christ to obtain your calling and election!* The wonderful experience of becoming a personal witness of Jesus Christ is independent of the salvation process. In this life, the witness of the Holy Ghost is a much more powerful event and testimony of our standing before God than any appearance in the physical world. This has been said many times by the prophets and apostles, yet the false notion continues to persist that in order to obtain your calling and election or even become a special witness of Jesus Christ a person must physically see and touch him. Again, this is *not* true!

> . . . The question frequently arises: 'Is it necessary for the members of the Council of the twelve to see the Savior in order to be an apostle?' It is their privilege to see him if occasion requires, but the Lord has taught that there is a stronger witness than seeing a personage, even of the Son of God, in a vision. I wish we could get this clear in the minds of the members of the Church . . . that seeing the Savior, does not leave as deep an impression in the mind as does the testimony of the Holy Ghost to the spirit.
>
> What is the lesson to be learned from this? That the impressions on the soul that come from the Holy Ghost are far more significant than a vision. It is where Spirit speaks to spirit, and the imprint upon the soul is far more difficult to erase. Every member of the Church should have the impressions on his soul made by the Holy Ghost that Jesus is the Son of God indelibly pictured so that they cannot be forgotten. (Joseph Fielding Smith, **Address to Seminary & Institute Faculty,** 1958)

2. *Many people believe you can be sealed to eternal life as an individual.* However, this is not true. You *can* receive your calling and election as an individual, but *you can only be sealed up to eternal life as a*

couple! Only after you and your spouse are bonded together in the eternal marriage covenant can you receive this final sealing ordinance—and only together.

Remember, when an individual is sealed to eternal life he is not just being sealed to the Celestial Kingdom but to the highest degree of the Celestial Kingdom! And a person cannot enter the highest degree of glory without first having been sealed for eternity to a husband or wife. You cannot be in the highest degree of the Celestial Kingdom alone!

> Then the revelation speaks of that obedience out of which eternal life grows, and still speaking both of celestial marriage and of making one's calling and election sure says: "Verily, verily, I say unto you, if a man marry a wife according to my word, and they are sealed by the Holy Spirit of promise, according to mine appointment" — that is, if they are both married and have their calling and election made sure — (Bruce R. McConkie, Doctrinal New Testament Commentary, Vol. 3, p. 345)

3. *Perhaps the most common and devastating misconception people have is that a person must be perfect in order to obtain their calling and election.* But this also is not true! *A person will still sin after being sealed to eternal life!*[1] The fact that you have obtained your election or testimony or that you have been sealed through an ordinance in the temple, or even that you have experienced the "second comforter" by having seen Jesus Christ personally, none of these monumental events mean that you no longer sin! You are not yet perfect, nor is this the end of your progression! There was only one sinless man on this earth: Jesus Christ. And even though we may have qualified for entrance into the Celestial Kingdom, it does not make us equal to our God! It might take thousands of years before we become perfect like He is. The sealing to eternal life simply gains us entrance into the Church of the Firstborn. And just as with new members of this earthly Church, our progress must continue!

[1] See Note 1

> *That all men commit sin, before and after baptism, and for that*
> *matter, before and after their calling and election is made sure,*
> *is self-evident. There has been only one Sinless One – the Lord*
> *Jesus who was God's own Son. (Bruce R. McConkie,* Doc-
> trinal New Testament Commentary, *3:75)*

4. Most members move through life with little or no understanding
    about their standing before God. They have no idea whether or
    not they are, or will be, worthy to enter the Celestial Kingdom.
    But many members of the Church are, and have been, completely
    faithful to the covenants they have made with God. They have al-
    ready completed all the requirements for obtaining their calling
    and election. Therefore, *it is possible to meet all the requirements to*
    obtain your calling and election and not know it! Perhaps the most
    amazing thing about the salvation process is the fact that many
    people who have already made all the sacrifices necessary to obtain
    this great blessing do not recognize it. And why wouldn't they
    know of such a great blessing that is within their reach? Because of
    lack of faith, or spiritual courage, or even something as simple as
    not taking the time to *ask* for this blessing to be bestowed upon
    them!

> *There are, of course, those whose callings and election have*
> *been made sure who have never exercised the faith nor exhib-*
> *ited the righteousness which would enable them to commune*
> *with the Lord on the promised basis. There are even those who*
> *neither believe nor know that it is possible to see the Lord in*
> *this day, and they therefore are without the personal incentive*
> *that would urge them onward in the pursuit of this consum-*
> *mation so devoutly desired by those with spiritual insight.*
> *(Bruce R. McConkie,* The Promised Messiah, *p. 586)*

5. *The greatest obstacle encountered by faithful members of the Church*
    who are striving to make their calling and election sure is lack of self-
    confidence. Many members of the Church simply do not believe it
    is possible for them to obtain their calling and election. This may
    be due to the false belief that a person must be perfect in order to

obtain this prize, or they may simply feel that they personally could never be worthy to enter the Celestial Kingdom. In any case, the biggest roadblock to their obtaining this great blessing is a simple lack of confidence in themselves.

In practice this self-deprecation is laughable! Most members of the Church can point to someone they *know* will make it to the Celestial Kingdom. Perhaps it is a leader in the church, a close family member, or even a neighbor—someone they have known and have seen live a Christ-like life every day and who is an obvious candidate for the Celestial Kingdom. Yet, if you asked those same righteous people if they thought they would make it to the Kingdom of Heaven, few would admit they might make it. To bring this into focus, let us ask one question: If the everyday, faithful members of the Church are not worthy to enter the Celestial Kingdom, who will be?

> *Christ is of course the perfect Prototype, the great Exemplar, the true Pattern for all men. But where among all the prophets and apostles, among all the saints and righteous persons of all the ages, can one find a better pattern, save Jesus only, than Paul? Here is a man who fought the truth, who persecuted the saints, on whose hands was found the blood of martyrs. And yet he enjoyed the gifts of the Spirit, worked out his salvation, made his calling and election sure, and has gone on to eternal exaltation in the mansions which are prepared. In effect, he is saying to Timothy, and through him to all of us, "If a blasphemer and perjurer, such as I, can be saved, what stands in your way?"* (Bruce R. McConkie, **Doctrinal** New Testament Commentary, 3:76)

CONCLUSION

As individuals, we must throw away our misconceptions about the path that leads to eternal life and our own inability to obtain the Celestial Kingdom. God did not create the plan of salvation simply to torture most of us by ensuring that only a select few of His children would make it back to live with Him! He is a loving and kind God that provided a way for *all* of his children to come back to his presence. The doctrine is not hard to understand and God is there to help us along our way. The key is to understand that at the same time we are finding and accepting the truth about God, we must also be willing to find and accept the truth about ourselves. If we have sinned, we need to repent. But if we have already repented and have begun to live a life of righteousness (not a perfect life, for that is impossible), we must develop the self confidence to see ourselves as God sees us—no longer as children stumbling around in the dark, but adults who in the light of divine knowledge have openly taken upon themselves sacred covenants in preparation for this specific event and blessing. If we finally come to understand what it really means to be a child of God, we will gain the confidence and understanding that as a child of God we have within ourselves the ability to become like him. We will finally cast away our fears and false humility and be able to stand with confidence before God and ask that this most precious blessing be given to us—to enter into His Kingdom and see God face to face.

> *What greater personal revelation could anyone receive than to see the face of his Maker? Is not this the crowning blessing of life? Can all the wealth compare with it? And is it an unseemly or unrighteous desire on man's part to hope and live and pray, all in such a way as to qualify for so great a manifestation? There is a true doctrine on these points, a doctrine unknown to many and unbelieved by more, a doctrine that is spelled out as specifically and extensively in the revealed word as are any of the other great revealed truths. There is no need for uncertainty or misunderstanding; and surely, if the Lord reveals a doctrine, we should seek to learn its principles and strive to apply them in our lives. This doctrine is: that mortal man, while in his flesh, has it in his power to see the Lord, to stand in his presence, to feel the nail marks in his hands and feet, and to receive from him such blessings as are reserved for those only who keep all his commandments and who are qualified for that eternal life which includes being in His presence forever. (Bruce R. McConkie,* A New Witness for the Articles of Faith*)*

NOTES

1. Bruce R. McConkie, *Doctrinal New Testament Commentary*, 3:75–76, 192.

"Thus in the revelation announcing the setting up of the restored church in this day, the Lord says: 'There is a possibility that man may fall from grace and depart from the living God; Therefore let the church take heed and pray always, lest they fall into temptation; Yea, and even let those who are sanctified take heed also.' (D&C 20:32–34.)

"Obviously the laws of repentance still apply, and the more enlightened a person is, the more he seeks the gift of repentance, and the harder he strives to free himself from sin as often as he falls short of the divine will and becomes subject in any degree to the Master of Sin who is Lucifer.

"And as a matter of fact, the added blessing of having one's calling and election made sure is itself an encouragement to avoid sin and a hedge against its further commission.

"Even though a person has his calling and election made sure and is sealed up unto eternal life, he still has his agency; he can still fall; he can still choose to serve Satan; but if he does—having had a perfect knowledge of the truth and now choosing to defy God; to trample his Son under foot; and to do despite to the Spirit of grace—he is damned eternally as a son of perdition."

Brigham Young, *Journal of Discourses,* 1:93.

"When we use the term perfection, it applies to man in his present condition, as well as to heavenly beings. We are now, or may be, as perfect in our sphere as God and angels are in theirs, but the greatest intelligence in existence can continually ascend to greater heights of perfection."

Chapter Four
Faith

We begin with faith. Faith is *the* most important and at the same time least understood doctrine of Christianity. All Christians have been taught about the power of faith through hearing and reading about the many miracles performed by Christ and his apostles in the Bible. Most Christians have also personally experienced this great power in their own lives through answers to prayer. God has permitted this great power to work through people even though they have little or no understanding of how and why it works. Faith is important because it is the power through which the entire universe was created and is now being upheld and sustained. Faith is also the power that men must obtain in order to inherit the Kingdom of God.

> *Faith, then, is the first great governing principle which has power, dominion, and authority over all things; by it they exist, by it they are upheld, by it they are changed, or by it they remain, agreeable to the will of God. Without it there is no power, and without power there could be no creation nor existence!* (Lectures on Faith, *Lecture 1, p. 8*)

SECTION 1: WHAT IS FAITH?

The first step in understanding faith is to define it. *What is faith?*

39

The scriptures have given us only a few specific definitions upon which we can draw:

Hebrews 11:1

"Faith is the substance (*assurance*) of things hoped for, the evidence (*proof*) of things not seen." (The italics are added; also see the footnotes in your scriptures)

1. Faith is an inward feeling, assurance, or *testimony* that things we hope for will come to pass. For example, even though we have no physical proof of Christ's resurrection, or that we will obtain the Kingdom of God Christ promised us, we can believe that they are true and hope that they will actually come to pass. Faith is when men gain an inward assurance that the promises made by God will, indeed, come to pass.

2. Faith is evidence, or *spiritual proof*, of the things we have been promised that have not yet come to pass. Once this assurance or testimony within us becomes strong enough, and we gain confidence that the things we have been taught are true, this same assurance or faith will give us the power to actually make it come to pass in our lives.

Alma 32:21

"And now as I said concerning faith—faith is not to have a perfect knowledge of things; therefore if ye have faith ye hope for things which are not seen, which are true."

3. Faith comes *before* we obtain a perfect knowledge of, or physical proof of, the things we believe in. It is important to understand that the development of faith must come *before* we obtain a sure knowledge or physical proof of the things we believe.

Fortunately, faith is much more empirical than many realize. It is evidence, though of things not seen. It is a stage in the evolution of evidence that precedes hard knowledge, as Alma points out so beautifully. (Alma 32.) We can actually experiment with gospel principles and accumulate our own personal evidence concerning the things experimented upon. We become our own witnesses as our minds expand and our souls swell. (Neal A. Maxwell, Deposition of a Disciple, pp. 64–65)

Ether 12:6

. . . faith is things which are hoped for and not seen; wherefore, dispute not because ye see not, for ye receive no witness until after the trial of your faith.

4. Physical, empirical proof of our faith (answers to prayer, gifts of the Spirit, or other miracles) cannot come until *after* we endure certain trials and sacrifices that test our faith. These trials are the key that turns our faith into power.

Faith is strongest when it is without illusions. Realistic faith alone provides allowance for the testing and proving dimensions of this mortal experience (D&C 98:12; Abraham 3:25). We undergo afflictions such as are "common to man" (1 Corinthians 10:13). Additionally, God will deliberately give us further lessons and experience which take us beyond the curriculum common to man and on into uncommon graduate studies or even post-doctoral discipleship. These trials are often the most difficult to bear. Our Father is full of pressing, tutorial love: "The Lord seeth fit to chasten his people; yea, he trieth their patience and their faith" (Mosiah 23:21). Nevertheless we are assured that "all these things shall give [us] experience, and shall be for [our] good," if we endure them well and learn from them (D&C 122:7; 121:8). For we are to learn much by our own experience. (Neal A. Maxwell, Not My Will, But Thine, pp. 4–5)

Ether 12:16

*Yea, and even all they who wrought miracles wrought them by
faith, even those who were before Christ and those who were
after.*

5. *All* miracles, gifts of the Spirit, answers to prayer, etc., which
become the empirical proof of what we believe, are the result
of the power of faith within us.

The Prophet Joseph Smith expanded this principle so we could
understand that faith was the basis of *all* action and power in the universe:

*From this we learn that faith is the assurance which men have
of the existence of things which they have not seen, and the
principle of action in all intelligent beings.*

*If men were duly to consider themselves, and turn their
thought and reflections to the operations of their own minds,
they would readily discover that it is faith, and faith only,
which is the moving cause of all action in them; that without it
both mind and body would be in a state of inactivity, and all
their exertions would cease, both physical and mental.*

*Were this class to go back and reflect upon the history of their
lives, from the period of their first recollection, and ask themselves what principle excited them to action, or what gave
them energy and activity in all their lawful avocations, callings, and pursuits, what would be the answer? Would it not
be that it was the assurance which they had of the existence of
things which they had not seen as yet? Was it not the hope
which you had, in consequence of your belief in the existence
of unseen things, which stimulated you to action and exertion
in order to obtain them? Would you exert yourselves to obtain
wisdom and intelligence, unless you did believe that you could
obtain them? Would you have ever sown, if you had not believed that you would reap? In a word, is there anything that
you would have done, either physical or mental, if you had not
previously believed? (Lectures on Faith, Lecture 1, pp. 7–8)*

Hebrews 11:3

> *Through faith we understand that the worlds were framed by*
> *the word of God . . . .*

6. Faith is the *power* through which God works.

The Prophet Joseph expanded our understanding of the power of
faith by explaining that faith was not just one of the powers that God
had, it was *the* power of God—there was no other power God used. It
was by and through the power of faith that all things were and are created. It is also through the power of faith that those creations are
maintained.

> *By this we understand that the principle of power which ex-*
> *isted in the bosom of God, by which the worlds were framed,*
> *was faith; and that it is by reason of this principle of power*
> *existing in the Deity, that all created things exist; so that all*
> *things in heaven, on earth, or under the earth exist by reason*
> *of faith as it existed in Him. (Lectures on Faith, Lecture 1, p. 8)*

Ether 12:18

> *And neither at any time hath any wrought miracles until after*
> *their faith; wherefore they first believed in the Son of God.*

7. Faith comes in and through the *belief in Jesus Christ* and the
    gospel principles he lived and taught. Christ is the way, the
    truth, and the life.[1] For those who seek and respond to the
    truth, Christ is the beginning and end of their search.

The Prophet Joseph taught that there were three things upon
which men should base their faith in order to make it valid. All three
are directly related to coming to know Jesus Christ, the kind of person
he was, and the kind of life he led.

---

[1] John 14:6

Let us here observe, that three things are necessary in order that any rational and intelligent being may exercise faith in God unto life and salvation. First, the idea that he actually exists. Secondly, a correct idea of his character, perfections, and attributes. Thirdly, an actual knowledge that the course of life which he is pursuing is according to his will. (Lectures on Faith, Lecture 3, p. 33)

To put it another way, in order to obtain faith, a person must be taught about Christ and learn to understand who and what God is. Then, he must live his life in a manner which will be acceptable to God. It is not enough to simply believe in the things we are taught by others. We must be certain that the doctrine we are taught is true and that the principles we learn are followed correctly and lived fully.

Let us review *what* faith is:

1. Faith is an inward assurance or *testimony* of things that the righteous hope for, such as the resurrection and living in the Kingdom of God.
2. Faith is an inward knowledge or *spiritual proof* that what we believe is true.
3. We must obtain this testimony *before* we can experience the miracles or empirical proof of the things we believe in.
4. Miracles, or empirical knowledge, can only come *after* our faith is tested.
5. When we obtain *empirical knowledge* of miracles, gifts of the Spirit, answers to prayers, etc., it is a direct result of our faith.
6. Faith is the *power* of God.
7. Faith must be based upon the knowledge and worship of *Jesus Christ.*

SECTION 2: HOW DO WE OBTAIN FAITH?

We have been talking about *what* faith is. Now we will discuss *how* a person obtains faith.

Alma 32:16

> *Therefore, blessed are they who humble themselves without being compelled to be humble; or rather, in other words, blessed is he that believeth in the word of God, and is baptized without stubbornness of heart, yea, without being brought to know the word, or even compelled to know, before they will believe.*

1. Being compelled to believe does not produce faith. Faith must develop as a result of men's agency, their willingness to *humble* themselves and choose to believe. The power of faith cannot be produced by outside force because it is a spiritual experience, an experience that happens inside of us. Therefore, the first thing a person must do in order to develop faith is to humble himself enough to invite the servants of God into his home and listen to their message with an open mind.

Romans 10:17

> *So then faith cometh by hearing, and hearing by the word of God.*

2. In order to obtain faith we first must be *taught* the gospel. In other words, we must obtain knowledge about God and eternal truth. This is the beginning of a circle of faith and knowledge that few understand. Most people have been taught and believe that when men obtain knowledge it does away with faith. But this is not true. Faith begins and ends with knowledge. Like all truth, faith is a circle.

> *How does the faith required as the first principle in the plan of salvation or gospel come? Let Paul answer: "So then faith cometh by hearing, and hearing by the word of God." (Romans 10:17) It is not the letter then that bringeth faith, but hearing the word of God dispensed by a living oracle or minister of God, clothed upon with power from on high. It is not a recorded gospel, but the preached word which emanates with*

power from a man of God inspired by the Holy Ghost. (John Taylor, The Gospel Kingdom, p. 332)

D&C 93:24, 28

And truth is knowledge of things as they are, and as they were, and as they are to come.

He that keepeth his commandments receiveth truth and light, until he is glorified in truth and knoweth all things.

3. In order to gain faith, we not only have to believe in and follow Christ, but we must be assured that everything we believe is the *truth.* Any falsehood or lies within our set of beliefs will not only detract from but will distort the truth we *do* have.

    Faith is based on truth and is preceded by knowledge. Until a person gains a knowledge of the truth he can have no faith. It follows that a knowledge of the true and living God is the beginning of faith unto life and salvation, "for faith could not center in a being of whose existence we have no idea, because the idea of his existence in the first instance is essential to the exercise of faith in him." (Lectures on Faith, p. 33)

    Not only is a true knowledge of God a condition precedent to the acquirement of this faith, but faith can be exercised only by those who conform to the principles of truth which come from the true God who actually exists. On this same principle no one can exercise faith . . . that does not conform to revealed truth, for no faith can be exercised "contrary to the plan of heaven." Faith is a gift of God bestowed as a reward for personal righteousness. It is always given when righteousness is present, and the greater the measure of obedience to God's laws the greater will be the endowment of faith. Hence the Prophet says that to acquire faith men must gain the actual knowledge "that the course of life which they pursue is according to the will of God, in order that they may be enabled to exercise faith in him unto life and salvation." (Bruce R. McConkie, Mormon Doctrine, pp. 262–264)

46

This principle of an ultimate search for the *truth* cannot be emphasized enough! Many people come to know that Jesus is the Christ, the Messiah, the Son of God. However, the gospel Christ taught has been changed and distorted over time—which has led to the creation of hundreds of different Christian sects, all teaching different doctrines. So in order to find the *truth,* a person must be willing to find and follow the truth wherever it can be found and wherever it may lead—even if it leads away from the doctrine that he currently believes or the church to which he belongs.

What is more important, being comfortable with your present belief system or knowing the truth?

You will need to answer that question for yourself, but for those who seek to return and live with God, finding and following the truth must trump everything else.

Alma 32:27

> But behold, if ye will awake and arouse your faculties, even to an experiment upon my words, and exercise a particle of faith, yea, even if ye can no more than desire to believe, let this desire work in you, even until ye believe in a manner that ye can give place for a portion of my words.

4. After hearing the Gospel, and in order to begin the process of developing faith, a person only needs to *desire* to believe the things that have been taught. This desire will lead a person to believe those sacred doctrines that ring true to him. It is desire that plants the seeds of truth brought by the servants of God that will in time produce the fruit of faith.

D&C 88:40

> For intelligence cleaveth unto intelligence; wisdom receiveth wisdom; truth embraceth truth; virtue loveth virtue; light

> *cleaveth unto light; mercy hath compassion on mercy and*
> *claimeth her own; justice continueth its course and claimeth*
> *its own; judgment goeth before the face of him who sitteth*
> *upon the throne and governeth and executeth all things.*

5. The principle or law through which the seeds of faith can be planted within someone's soul is the natural, eternal law of *attraction*. People who seek the truth will attract, understand, and embrace the truth. People who desire to know the truth will be willing to invite the servants of God into their homes, will listen to the doctrine they teach, and will accept their teachings because they will recognize the truth and want to live it.

Have you ever wondered why some people can understand and accept the truth and some can't or won't? The reason people can recognize the truth in this life is that all men lived as spirit beings in a life before this. (In fact, a person's ability to learn *anything* is based upon this same principle.) All people lived as spirits with God in a premortal life, where they learned the truth of all things. After coming to this mortal existence and obtaining a physical body, people's ability to understand and accept the truth is directly related to how faithfully they learned and lived these same truths in the pre-mortal life. It is actually very simple: those who were faithful in the premortal life will understand and accept the truth more easily in this life. This is the reason that Christ could be so confident in saying: "My sheep hear my voice, and I know them, and they follow me."[2] Christ knew that all who knew him and followed him in the pre-mortal life would recognize him again in this life. In fact, many of the great spiritual leaders from history (Christ, Confucius, Martin Luther, Abraham Lincoln, etc.) were considered the "noble and great ones" from the premortal life[3] whom God chose to be the leaders and examples in this life, and as a direct result of their personal obedience and faithfulness in the life before this.

---

[2] John 10:27
[3] Abraham 3:22

*When men begin to live by faith they begin to draw near to
God; and when faith is perfected they are like Him; and because He is saved they are saved also; for they will be in the
same situation He is in, because they have come to Him; and
when He appears they shall be like Him, for they will see Him
as He is. (Lectures on Faith, Lecture 7, p. 63)*

2 Nephi 33:1

*. . . for when a man speaketh by the power of the Holy Ghost
the power of the Holy Ghost carrieth it unto the hearts of the
children of men.*

6. After hearing the gospel taught by the power of the Holy
   Ghost dwelling within the servants of God, people will *feel* the
   truth of their words by and through that same power. These
   spiritual feelings, produced in part by the very presence of the
   servants of God, are the seeds that will eventually produce
   faith.[4]

Alma 32:17-18

*Yea, there are many who do say: If thou wilt show unto us a
sign from heaven, then we shall know of a surety; then we
shall believe. Now I ask, is this faith? Behold, I say unto you,
Nay; for if a man knoweth a thing he hath no cause to believe,
for he knoweth it.*

7. *Signs*, or physical, empirical evidence, cannot produce faith.
   Remember what we learned about faith: faith must precede
   knowledge. If we see miracles or empirical evidence of the
   truth *before* we have a chance to have our beliefs properly
   formed and tested, we will never be able to develop the power
   of faith. This is the reason that Satan's plan was rejected in the
   premortal life. He wanted to take away men's agency so he

---

[4] D&C 50:21–22

could force all men to return to heaven. God knew this plan would not work because it would not produce the faith required to be able to live with God once we returned to Him.

John 7:17

> *If any man will do his will, he shall know of the doctrine, whether it be of God, or whether I speak of myself.*

8. In order to turn our belief into knowledge, we are required to *live* the principles that have been taught. Faith without works is dead because unless we move our thoughts or beliefs into action we will never witness the physical, empirical proof of our faith. We will never see or experience answers to prayer, gifts of the Spirit, or miracles. We can never obtain the perfect knowledge spoken of by Alma that is necessary to see the face of God and live.

Let us review how people obtain faith:

1. A person must *humble* himself and be willing to listen and learn from the servants of God.
2. A person is *taught* the gospel of Jesus Christ.
3. The information taught and received must be the *truth*.
4. A person must develop a *desire* to believe.
5. The law of *attraction* will permit the truth to be understood and accepted.
6. The person will begin to develop faith as he *feels* the Spirit and accepts the truth.
7. *Signs* never develop faith.
8. Faith can only turn into knowledge when we *live* the principles we have been taught.

As we study *what* faith is and *how* faith is obtained, we can each learn to develop faith in our individual lives. Gaining faith is the first step required by God to gain entrance into His kingdom. When we plant the seeds of faith and faithfully do what it takes to make them grow, they will bear celestial fruit. After we have tasted the fruits of faith (miracles, gifts of the Spirit, answers to prayer), we will be ready for the next step in our progression.

Here is the process of developing faith:

1. Servants of God teach us about Christ and the Kingdom of God.
2. Desiring to obtain the promises we have been taught, we begin to believe.
3. As our belief grows, we begin to obtain an inner feeling, assurance, or testimony that the things we believe are actually true.
4. Over time our newly developed faith is tested, and we must endure trials to prove we are willing to live by the things we believe. If we prove ourselves and endure, our faith becomes powerful.
5. The power we obtain from faith can be used to perform miracles, experience the gifts of the Spirit, and eventually help us obtain all of the promises we have been hoping for. These miracles give us physical, empirical proof of our faith—they turn our faith into perfect knowledge.

The Prophet Alma explained this same process in his parable of the seed (Alma 32:28–43):

1. A person is willing to listen to the servants of God, willing to "experiment" on their words.
2. A seed is planted in his heart because of his desire to believe what is said.
3. If what is said is true, it begins to "swell within your breasts" and gives an inner feeling or assurance that what has been taught is true.
4. If a person continues to believe in spite of the tests and trials of life, the seed continues to grow.

51

5. As his faith or "tree" grows, it begins to bring forth fruit, physical proof of the inner faith he has been developing. This process gives him "perfect knowledge."

You now should have a basic understanding of what faith is: an inner feeling or testimony of the things we believe. But it is not enough to believe in just *any* doctrine taught to us (after all, men can and will believe almost anything!). It is just as important that what we believe is the *truth*. There are hundreds, even thousands of different religions in the world today, all containing some doctrines that are true and some that are false. It is not enough to believe in *some* things that are true; we must make sure that *all* of the things we believe are true. This is part of the test men experience in this mortal life: whether or not they can discern truth from error. Then, once men know the truth, they must choose whether or not they will live it.

In order to obtain the kind of faith that develops *power*, our belief system must be based upon two things: knowledge concerning *Jesus Christ*, and the search for *eternal truth*. It does us no good to believe in and follow doctrines that are false, because in the end our faith will develop no proof, no evidence, and therefore will not develop the power to bring to pass what we hope for. We must be willing to test our beliefs to see if they are true. The ability to test our faith will weed out false doctrines and produce the physical proof or miracles that lead to "perfect knowledge." Then, when we *know* that what we believe in is true, we will be prepared to see the face of God and live.

SECTION 3: THE CIRCLE OF FAITH AND KNOWLEDGE

One of the stumbling blocks people have to overcome in their understanding of faith is the idea that once a person obtains perfect knowledge of a doctrine, their faith disappears. The Prophet Alma taught that after our knowledge of the truth becomes "perfect" our faith becomes "dormant" (Alma 32:34). Many people have read Alma's discourse on faith and assume that we have faith only and until we obtain sure knowledge by seeing or experiencing something that proves to us that our faith is true. Once we obtain this sure knowledge we no longer need or have faith, because we have a sure knowledge. But this is an incorrect interpretation of this doctrine and is easily proven to be false. Consider the following:

1. God knows all things, or all the laws in the universe.

   O how great the holiness of our God! For he knoweth all things and there is not anything save he knows it. (2 Nephi 9:20)

2. God created the world by the power of His faith.

   Through faith we understand that the worlds were framed by the word of God . . . (Hebrews 11:3)

If God knows all things and knowledge destroys or takes the place of faith, then how can we explain that faith is the power God uses to create? If faith is done away by knowledge, then God would not have any need for faith. But we know this is not true: God has faith, needs faith, and uses faith. Then what *is* the relationship between faith and knowledge? This is one of the most important concepts concerning faith.

Remember that the first step in obtaining faith is to obtain *knowledge* of God.[5] So knowledge of the gospel must precede faith. We receive knowledge of God by listening to the servants of God who pass on the knowledge they have received. This knowledge we receive about God is *spiritual knowledge*. It is spiritual because it is not something we can see, taste, etc. Since faith is something we cannot prove, it is different from *physical knowledge* like the kind we would obtain using the usual empirical means. Faith,then, is an accumulation of spiritual knowledge. In fact, we could say that *faith is spiritual knowledge*.

The process of faith is a circle: we obtain knowledge of God in order to develop faith. Then, as our spiritual knowledge grows, our faith

[5] Romans 10:17

53

develops the power to make our righteous hopes and desires real: we can produce miracles, use the gifts of the Spirit, or see the face of God and live. This is what Alma calls "perfect knowledge." Perfect knowledge is obtained when we have empirical proof that our faith is real. In addition, perfect knowledge is retained in our memory, an experience we will then use to increase our faith in other doctrines in which we only yet believe. We can then use these experiences, this perfect knowledge, to motivate us to greater works and therefore, greater knowledge. As our knowledge and faith grow to the point of having a perfect knowledge of *all* things, we can become like God—knowing all things and having the power to create worlds.

> To gain faith men must first have knowledge; then as their faith increases, they come to a state where it is supplanted by perfect knowledge; and in any field in which perfect knowledge has been gained, "faith is dormant." (Alma 32:21-34) For instance, a man first comes to a knowledge of the nature and kind of being that Christ is, and he thereby is enabled to gain faith in him. As a result he gains further knowledge about Christ as an effect of faith and by revelation from the Holy Ghost. This knowledge and this faith both increase, supplementing each other, until by the power of faith the veil is rent, the man sees Christ and gains a perfect knowledge of him. Then, as Alma expresses it, "in that thing" his "faith is dormant" (Alma 32:34), although in other things his faith may not yet have blossomed forth into perfect knowledge.

> The Brother of Jared is one who followed this course until he saw the Lord. Wherefore, having this perfect knowledge of God, he could not be kept from within the veil, therefore he saw Jesus; and he did minister unto him. Indeed, "The Lord could not withhold anything from him, for he knew that the Lord could show him all things." (Ether 3:19-26) (Bruce R. McConkie, **Mormon Doctrine,** p. 267 FAITH)

> The gifts of faith are two: knowledge and power. These are to each other as the sides of a shield. Where one is, there is the other. Faith is knowledge that transcends ordinary boundaries. Such high knowledge is built upon human experience. It sums

up all that existence has taught. In communion with God, in prayer, the offering of life's results is transmitted into faith. Thus, faith is all of man's knowledge plus divine interpretation. Human knowledge is as the chrysalis, with the larva within; faith is as the butterfly, with its dead prison behind. Such knowledge knows no doubt, for no scaffolding is needed where truth stands fully revealed. (Joseph Fielding Smith, The Restoration of All Things, p. 189)

Faith is based on past experience. It is not blind obedience, even without total understanding, to follow a Father who has proved himself. (The Teachings of Spencer W. Kimball, p. 59)

The important thing to understand is that there are two types of knowledge: *spiritual knowledge* and *physical or empirical knowledge.* In order for our faith to develop into perfect knowledge, we must progress to the point of obtaining physical knowledge, or miracles. Our spiritual faith must produce tangible fruit.

"Miracles are the fruits of faith," the Prophet said on another occasion. "Faith comes by hearing the word of God. If a man has not faith enough to do one thing, he may have faith to do another: if he cannot remove a mountain, he may heal the sick. Where faith is there will be some of the fruits: all gifts and power which were sent from heaven, were poured out on the heads of those who had faith. (History of the Church, vol. 5, p. 355.)" (Bruce R. McConkie, Mormon Doctrine, pp. 264–266 FAITH)

Once we have progressed to the point of experiencing physical or empirical knowledge about the things we spiritually believe to be true, our knowledge becomes perfect. Picture it this way: in the same way our body cannot become perfect until our spirit and physical body are united together in the resurrection, our knowledge of God cannot become perfect until our spiritual knowledge and physical knowledge are united.

Chapter Five
A New Paradigm of Faith

If we bring together some of the new definitions and understandings about faith, we can create a more realistic picture of what faith is and how faith works.

1. *Spiritual knowledge is faith.* It is one and the same thing. When truth is understood and fully accepted, it turns into a power the scriptures calls faith.

> *Faith is borne of knowledge and matures through righteousness. To gain faith unto life and salvation, men must first adopt the concept that God actually exists; they must have a correct idea of his character, perfections, and attributes; and they must obtain an actual knowledge that the course of life they are pursuing is according to his omnipotent will.* (Bruce R. McConkie, The Mortal Messiah, Vol. 3, p. 265)

> *Queries: Which comes first faith or knowledge?*
> *Answers: Faith is the child of knowledge. It is reserved for those only who first have knowledge; there neither is nor can be any faith until there is knowledge. No one can have faith in a God of whom he knows nothing. Faith is founded on truth; it is the offspring of truth; it can never exist alone and apart from the truth. No one can have faith unto life and salvation in a false god; no idol ever had power to raise the dead or stop the sun. And faith is power. It is true that faith in*

*some doctrine or on some theological point may be imperfect;
it is true that sproutings of either faith or knowledge can become perfect relative to that doctrine or concept. But faith itself — the great and eternal power that creates and governs and
saves, faith unto life and salvation — saving faith grows out of
knowledge and cannot come in any other way.*

*"Faith cometh by hearing," Paul says, "and hearing the word
of God" taught by the power of the Holy Ghost. (Romans
10:17). Faith comes to those only who receive the word of
truth. The gospel embraces all truth, and truth — nothing
else — can bring salvation.*

*Truth, diamond truth, is the rock foundation upon which faith
rests, and no one can have faith in God or in any gospel truth
unless and until he comes to a knowledge of whatever truth is
involved.*

*Knowing, then, that knowledge precedes faith, that faith is
founded on truth, and that falsehood and error do not and cannot exercise any saving power, we are led to the inevitable
conclusion that faith cannot be exercised contrary to the order
of heaven. It takes the power of God (which is faith!) to bring
to pass the immortality and eternal life of man. All progress,
all science, all religion, even life itself, exist and are because of
truth. And faith can only be exercised in conformity with true
principles. (Bruce R. McConkie,* A New Witness for the Articles of Faith, *pp. 166–168)*

2. *Spiritual knowledge, when lived and followed correctly, creates
    empirical knowledge.* This is evidence of spiritual things in the
    real, physical world. This "real world" knowledge appears in
    the forms of miracles, priesthood ordinances (such as healing,
    baptism, temple endowments, etc.), gifts of the Spirit, answers
    to prayer, etc.

    *Miracles, signs, the gifts of the Spirit, the knowledge of God
    and godliness, and every conceivable good thing — all these are
    the effects of faith; all of these come because faith has become
    the ruling force in the lives of the saints. Conversely, where*

> these things are not, faith is not . . . A man who has none of
> the gifts has no faith; and he deceives himself, if he supposes he
> has. (TPJS, p. 270)

3. *When our spiritual knowledge (faith) becomes real (miracles, gifts
   of the Spirit, etc.), we obtain a perfect knowledge.* Just as we become perfect when our spirit and body are united in the resurrection, our knowledge becomes perfect when our temporal
   knowledge (miracles) confirm our spiritual knowledge (faith).
   At this point, our faith becomes dormant or united with reality.

> *In the eternal sense, because faith is the power of God himself,
> it embraces within its fold a knowledge of all things. This
> measure of faith, the faith by which the worlds are and were
> created and which sustains and upholds all things, is found
> only among resurrected persons. It is the faith of saved beings.
> But mortals are in process, through faith, of gaining eternal
> salvation. Their faith is based on a knowledge of the truth,
> within the meaning of Alma's statement that "faith is not to
> have a perfect knowledge of things," but that men have faith
> when they "hope for things which are not seen, which are
> true." In this sense faith is both preceded and supplanted by
> knowledge, and when any person gains a perfect knowledge on
> any given matter, then, as pertaining to that thing, he has
> faith no longer; or, rather, his faith is dormant; it has been
> supplanted by pure knowledge. (See Alma 32:21-34.)* (Bruce
> R. McConkie, A New Witness for the Articles of Faith, *pp.*
> 169–210)

Let us give you some specific examples of how this process works.

Example 1: The doctrine of *prayer:*
1. A man is taught by the missionaries about prayer.
2. He desires to believe what he has been taught is true.
3. As he develops a feeling of trust about the doctrine, he desires
   to prove that the doctrine is true; he wants to change his belief
   into knowledge.

4. Understanding that in order to *know* whether the doctrine is true he must keep the commandments and live a righteous life, he begins to do so.
5. The man begins to pray in earnest in an attempt to receive an answer to his prayers.
6. After a period of testing, the Lord answers the man's prayers.
7. The answer is *proof* that there is a God and that prayer really works.
8. The man now *knows* that prayer is a true doctrine. He has obtained a perfect knowledge about prayer because he used his spiritual knowledge (faith) to obtain a physical knowledge (answer to his prayers), which created a perfect knowledge.
9. This perfect knowledge about prayer increases his faith about the other doctrines he has been taught by the missionaries, and motivates him to gain a perfect knowledge of the other doctrines he has been taught.

Example 2: One of the gifts of the Spirit; *healing.*

1   Using the process followed above, after learning of the gifts of the Spirit—and having both a desire and a need to be healed—the man requests a blessing at the hands of the elders.
2. According to his faith, the man is healed.
3. In the act of being healed, the man obtains *proof* that spiritual gifts exist and that men can heal by the power of faith and the use of the priesthood.
4. Now the man *knows* that the gifts of the Spirit, and specifically healing, are real. He has obtained a perfect knowledge about the gift of healing.
5. This perfect knowledge increases his faith and motivates him to continue to study and pray, continue to keep the commandments, and develop a desire to serve others in the same manner.

Example 3: The story of the Brother of Jared (Ether 3:6–20)

1. Because of his faith, Jared prays to the Lord, expecting an answer. When the Lord answers his prayer, he gains knowledge. As his knowledge grows, his faith is magnified and he sees the finger of the Lord, gaining a more perfect knowledge (verses 6–9).
2. With his increased faith, he *asks* to see the Lord face to face (verse 10).
3. Because of his perfect knowledge that God lives, he is redeemed from the fall. He is permitted back into the presence of God (verses 11–16).
4. His faith led to knowledge, which led to a *perfect* knowledge. Because of his knowledge, he could not be kept from seeing Christ (verses 19–20).

Most of you reading this book have already experienced the reality of God—perhaps more than once. Whether as answers to prayers or experiencing the gifts of the Spirit, most people have already obtained a portion of this perfect knowledge to one degree or another. Take *any* doctrine, *any* gift of the Spirit, *any* eternal truth contained in the gospel of Jesus Christ and follow this same process, and a person can obtain a perfect knowledge of that doctrine or truth. After a man obtains a perfect knowledge of *all* truth, he will become like God.

It is important to understand that faith without righteous actions (or "works" as used in the Bible) is dead. If we obtain spiritual knowledge (faith) and never test that knowledge by keeping the commandments or praying or doing those things that will result in obtaining physical manifestations of the Spirit (such as miracles, gifts of the Spirit, answers to prayer, etc.), we will never obtain the perfect knowledge or power necessary to see the face of God and live. We will never be prepared to live in the kingdom of God. We will never receive the reward we seek: the Celestial Kingdom and eternal life.

The same is true in reverse. If we seek for signs or physical manifestations of God before developing faith, we may be permitted to see them, but we will never develop the faith and power necessary to burst the veil of heaven and see our Lord and Savior. In fact, signs will have just the opposite effect. If we seek and see signs, it will harden our hearts and we will refuse to do the things necessary to obtain salvation, because we will feel we already "know" everything.

> *And he that seeketh signs shall see signs, but not unto salvation. Verily, I say unto you, there are those among you who seek signs, and there have been such even from the beginning; but, behold, faith cometh not by signs, but signs follow those that believe. Yea, signs come by faith, not by the will of men, not as they please, but by the will of God. (D&C 63:7–10)*

The spirit and the flesh must be united to become perfect. Faith (spiritual knowledge) without works (temporal actions) is dead, because only by uniting the two can we become perfect.

James 2:14–26

> *What does it profit, my brethren, though a man say he hath faith, and have not works? Can faith save him? If a brother or sister be naked, and destitute of daily food, and one of you say unto them, Depart in peace, be ye warmed and filled: notwithstanding ye give them not those things which are needful to the body; what doth it profit? Even so faith, if it hath not works, is dead, being alone.*

> *Thou believest that there is one God; thou doest well: the devils also believe, and tremble. But wilt thou know, O vain man, that faith without works is dead?*

> *Was not Abraham our father justified by works, when he had offered Isaac his son upon the altar? Seest thou how faith wrought with his works, and by works was faith made perfect?*

> *For as the body without the spirit is dead, so faith without works is dead also.*

And what are the works or actions that men must perform in order to make their faith perfect? There are three things that God has directed man to do to make our faith manifest in the flesh and thereby obtain the perfect knowledge that we seek.

1. Keep the commandments.

    He that hath my commandments, and keepeth them, he it is that loveth me: and he that loveth me shall be loved of my Father, and I will love him, and will manifest myself unto him. (John 14:21)

    Verily, thus saith the Lord: It shall come to pass that every soul who forsaketh his sins and cometh unto me, and calleth on my name, and obeyeth my voice, and keepeth my commandments, shall see my face and know that I am. (D&C 93:1)

2. Serve our fellow man.

    And behold, I tell you these things that ye may learn wisdom; that ye may learn that when ye are in the service of your fellow beings ye are only in the service of your God. (Mosiah 2:17)

3. Obtain the Priesthood ordinances of God.

    And this greater priesthood administereth the gospel and holdeth the key of the mysteries of the kingdom, even the key of the knowledge of God. Therefore, in the ordinances thereof, the power of godliness is manifest. And without the ordinances thereof, and the authority of the priesthood, the power of godliness is not manifest unto men in the flesh; for without this no man can see the face of God, even the Father, and live. (D&C 84:19–22)

It is through temporal, earthly ordinances and gifts of the Spirit that the power of God is made manifest in the flesh. Without these ordinances and gifts, no man would be able to show his faith in the real world. He would therefore never receive perfect knowledge and never be able to see the face of God.

These three branches of earthly works are absolutely necessary in order to transition from faith (spiritual knowledge) to perfect knowledge: our ability to witness miracles, spiritual gifts, etc., which are the physical, empirical proof of our faith. Without our being obedient to God, keeping the commandments, fulfilling our church callings, and living a Christian life, there can be no changing our simple faith into power, no development of the perfect knowledge that opens the veil of heaven. It is truly a correct doctrine that faith without works is dead.

> *We know that faith is a gift of God; it is the fruitage of righteous living. It does not come to us by our command, but is the result of doing the will of our Heavenly Father. If we lack faith, let us examine ourselves to see if we have been keeping His commandments, and repent without delay if we have not.* (George Albert Smith, **Sharing the Gospel With Others,** *p. 49*)

Precept upon precept: Eternal Progression

As we progress, we obtain a perfect knowledge in degrees, one step at a time, until we have a perfect knowledge of all things that are true. As children of God, we must continue to progress precept upon precept, adding one piece of knowledge to another until we obtain all knowledge, all truth. This process will not, cannot, be accomplished in this life alone; it will take long after we are resurrected, perhaps eons, to obtain the same position our Lord and Savior was able to obtain immediately after his resurrection and glorification. However, eternal progression does reach the point where, if we continue on the path laid out by Jesus Christ, we will know all things. The ultimate circle will be completed. Like Christ, we too will know the beginning and the end; we too will be like God, an Alpha and Omega, fulfilling our ultimate destiny as children of God the Eternal Father.

If thou shalt ask, thou shalt receive revelation upon revelation, knowledge upon knowledge, that thou mayest know the mysteries and peaceable things – that which bringeth joy, that which bringeth life eternal. (D&C 42:61)

For behold, thus saith the Lord God: I will give unto the children of men line upon line, precept upon precept, here a little and there a little; and blessed are those who hearken unto my precepts, and lend an ear unto my counsel, for they shall learn wisdom; for unto him that receiveth I will give more; and from them that shall say, We have enough, from them shall be taken away even that which they have. (2 Nephi 28:30)

God's guarantee to His children

To some who lack desire, the process of obtaining faith might seem overwhelming. But God has promised us two things to ensure that this process of developing faith and obtaining perfect knowledge will *always* work; two ways that people are *guaranteed* to be able to obtain perfect knowledge and move their faith into the real world:

1. God has promised *all* his children (no matter to what church they belong or what they currently believe) that he will answer their prayers.

    And when ye shall receive these things, I would exhort you that ye would ask God, the Eternal Father, in the name of Christ, if these things are not true; and if ye shall ask with a sincere heart, with real intent, having faith in Christ, he will manifest the truth of it unto you, by the power of the Holy Ghost. And by the power of the Holy Ghost ye may know the truth of all things. (Moroni 10:4,5)

2. God has promised *every* faithful member of his church a gift of the Spirit, so he is assured of experiencing the power of God manifest in the flesh: a physical earthly sign of the reality of our spiritual knowledge, insuring that we obtain at least one

65

piece of perfect knowledge. In fact, we are told that we are to be given this gift as a means to prevent our being deceived by false doctrine, knowing that only the truth can be made manifest in the real world.

Wherefore, beware lest ye are deceived; and that ye may not be deceived seek ye earnestly the best gifts, always remembering for what they are given: for verily I say unto you, they are given for the benefit of those who love me and keep my commandments, and him that seeketh so to do; that all may be benefitted that seek or ask of me, that ask and not for a sign that they may consume it upon their lusts.

For all have not every gift given unto them; for there are many gifts, and to every man is given a gift by the Spirit of God. (D&C46:8, 9, 11)

It is important to understand that miracles follow those who believe. If a person has not had a true spiritual experience, they do not have faith. This may seem like a harsh statement, but it is true nonetheless. The testimony of God is brought to the hearts of men by the Holy Ghost, and the Holy Ghost facilitates the production of spiritual experiences and miracles, the basis for a person's testimony of the gospel. In fact, no one can have a true testimony of Christ without first having some kind of spiritual experience! Joseph Smith said: "No man can receive the Holy Ghost without receiving revelations. The Holy Ghost is a revelator" (TPJS p. 328). And Paul said that "no man can say that Jesus is the Lord, but by the Holy Ghost" (1 Corinthians 12:3). One way or another, the only way to tell whether a person is a true believer and has faith in Christ is to determine whether their faith has produced a spiritual witness or miracle.

How does the *power* of faith actually work?

We have learned how men obtain faith, but how do men *use* the faith they have? How do we obtain answers to our prayers, heal the sick, prophesy, or obtain any physical manifestation of our spiritual knowledge? Since faith is spiritual knowledge, faith works by mental or spiritual exertion.

*"We ask, then, what are we to understand by a man's work-
ing by faith? We answer — we understand that when a man
works by faith he works by mental exertion instead of physical
force. It is by words, instead of exerting his physical powers,
with which every being works when he works by faith. God
said, 'Let there be light, and there was light.' Faith, then,
works by words; and with these its mightiest works have been,
and will be, performed."* (Lectures on Faith, *Lecture 6, p. 59*)

Faith can be developed and used by *anyone* at any time. This is
why members of other churches can and do experience such fruits of
faith as miracles and answers to prayer. The spiritual gifts and blessings
experienced by people of other faiths are not a result of the power of
Satan (as some may believe in an attempt to bolster their own belief
system). They are a direct result of eternal laws that apply to *everyone*,
not just the limited number of people who claim membership in
Christ's true church.

*Faith is an eternal principle, an eternal law; it is built into the
universe itself as a governing, controlling force; it is ordained
of God and shall endure forever. It takes no special divine decree to cause the effects of the law of gravity to be manifest
everywhere on earth at all times. The law has been established
and the effects that flow from it are everlastingly the same. So
it is with faith. He who has given a law unto all things has
established faith as the power and force by which he and his
shall operate in righteousness forever. No special divine decree
is needed to utilize the power of faith; it is like gravity: any-
time any person in any age conforms to the law involved, the
ordained results will attend.* (Bruce R. McConkie, **The Mortal Messiah,** *Vol. 2, p. 287*)

How then do we use our faith? How can we learn to use this great
power within us? First, we must ask God in the name of Christ. We
have been told specifically to "seek ye earnestly the best gifts;"[1] we
have been told specifically to ask so we can receive. God wants us to
develop our faith. He wants us to gain the perfect knowledge of which

---

[1] D&C 46:8

67

we have spoken. It is part of His eternal plan for His children, so He will do whatever he can to ensure our success.

> *To ask is one thing; to seek is a greater thing; and to knock at the very doors of heaven assures that those holy portals will be opened and that the desired blessings will be forthcoming. Those who take no thought save it be to ask are denied the blessing. 'Let him ask of God . . . But let him ask in faith' is the divine decree (James 1:5–6; D&C 9:7–9). Nothing is withheld from those who seek the Lord with all their heart. Those whose search falls short of the utmost bounds to which it should extend shall not find the desired treasure.* (Bruce R. McConkie, The Mortal Messiah, *Vol. 3, p. 188)*

What does this mean? It means that when we pray for an answer or a blessing we must do so with great desire and *intensity*! It is not enough to say our prayers like we did as children: "Now I lay me down to sleep . . . ." We must consciously increase the power and mental exertion of our thoughts so that we can break through the veil of heaven and insure our prayers are both heard *and* answered! This is not easy. It takes great desire and effort for someone to pray "with all their heart." But if we truly desire to *know*, if we really need that blessing from God, then our faith will be effective and we will receive the desired result.

> *How do men exercise faith? What are we to understand by a man's working by faith?*
>
> *Those who work by faith must first have faith; no one can use a power that he does not possess, and the faith or power must be gained by obedience to those laws upon which its receipt is predicated. Those who work by faith must believe in the Lord Jesus Christ and in his Father. They must accept at face value what the revealed word teaches as to the character, attributes, and perfections of the Father and the Son. They must then work the works of righteousness until they know within themselves that their way of life conforms to the divine will, and they must be willing to lay their all on the altar of the Almighty.*

And then — when the day is at hand and the hour has arrived
for the miracle to be wrought — then they must be in tune with
the Holy Spirit of God. He who is the Author of faith, he
whose power faith is, He whose works are the embodiment of
justice and judgment and wisdom and all good things, even
He must approve the use of his power in the case at hand.
Faith cannot be exercised contrary to the order of heaven or
contrary to the will and purposes of Him whose power it is.
Men work by faith when they are in tune with the Spirit and
when what they seek to do by mental exertion and by the spo-
ken word is the mind and will of the Lord. (Bruce R. McCon-
kie, A New Witness for the Articles of Faith, *p.191–192)*

There is a misunderstanding concerning the power of faith. Christ said that if people had faith as small as a grain of mustard seed, a person would be able to move mountains.[2] Upon reading this, most people feel that Christ is criticizing them for their lack of faith; after all, they have never moved mountains or experienced great miracles! But Christ meant something else entirely. Christ was giving people a glimpse of what was possible with the faith they already had inside of them.

Most Christians already have faith. They have *proven* their faith by their works—attending church, being baptized and accepting Jesus as their Savior and Messiah, and attempting to live a righteous life. These actions have *already* produced faith within the person! The problem does not lie in their lack of faith, but in their inability to use their faith properly. Christ's words and admonition to everyone is this: If a person can move mountains with faith as small as a mustard seed, just think of what he can do with the large amount of faith he already has! Many more people have faith than use faith.

CONCLUSION

Faith is an act of will on the part of man. It is part of our personal obligation as children of God to seek after God. It is our responsibility

---

[2] Matthew 17:20

to find the truth and accept it once it is found. It is our duty to live the truth we know and understand. It is not God's responsibility to save us—Christ has already completed this work—it is our responsibility to work out our salvation with fear and trembling.[3] But God is ready to help us. He has placed within us the ability to know the truth when we hear it and will give everyone the opportunity to hear the gospel and accept or reject it. But in the end, it is up to each and every one of us to choose whether we will follow the path of truth and righteousness or turn away from the opportunities given us and suffer the eternal consequences.

---

[3] Phillippians 2:12

Chapter Six
The Key to Eternal Life: The Law of Sacrifice

The gospel of Jesus Christ is a lifestyle. It begins with small steps of faith, such as taking the missionary discussions, getting baptized, and accepting your first church calling. It culminates with strength and power as we participate in the temple ordinances and learn to make the ultimate sacrifice, the consecration of all earthly things, including our own life if necessary, for the advancement of the Kingdom of God on earth.

The plan of salvation is the path to our own perfection. It is the process through which we gain spiritual power. Specifically, it is a series of covenants or promises that each person must make in order to enter the Celestial Kingdom. No one who hopes to live with God the Father is exempt from these steps. Not one man, woman, or child will ever enter the highest Kingdom of Glory without taking upon themselves the necessary covenants, and proving they have the courage and will to live them. Even Jesus Christ himself— the great Jehovah, creator of heaven and earth, and the only perfect man that has ever lived— was not exempt from these requirements.

There are eternal laws that must be followed and fulfilled in order for us to reach the Celestial Kingdom. God is a just god, and no respecter of persons, because anyone who lives these laws will enter the

Kingdom of God. God is required by law to accept anyone who keeps the commandments and fulfills these laws.

> *I the Lord, am bound when ye do what I say; but when ye do not what I say, ye have no promise. (D&C 82:10)*

God is also prevented from receiving anyone who willfully disobeys His laws.

> *But there is a law given, and a punishment affixed, and a repentance granted; which repentance, mercy claimeth; otherwise, justice claimeth the creature and executeth the law, and the law inflicteth the punishment; if not so, the works of justice would be destroyed, and God would cease to be God. What, do ye suppose that mercy can rob justice? I say unto you, Nay; not one whit. If so, God would cease to be God. (Alma 42:22, 25)*

There is, and can be, no favoritism in the gospel plan, because it is based upon eternal laws and covenants between God and man.

As we progress along the path and prove ourselves by keeping these covenants and serving God, we prepare ourselves to make an "ultimate" sacrifice. Just as we have followed Christ though the exalting steps of faith, baptism, and the cleansing power of the Holy Ghost, we must follow Him in the fulfilling of the law of sacrifice.

From the beginning, God has shown that personal sacrifice is necessary to obtain real faith and spiritual power: Adam and Eve sacrificed living in paradise in order to fulfill the plan of salvation; Noah sacrificed his good name to build a boat in the middle of a desert; Abraham sacrificed his precious son, Isaac; Moses sacrificed power and prestige and took up the unbearable burden of wayward Israel; Job was reduced to a sickly, diseased, and homeless man in order to prove the power of his testimony; Lehi and Ishmael left home and country; Abinadi was burned at the stake for testifying of King Noah's wickedness; Alma and the sons of Mosiah left friends and families for over 14 years to preach to the Lamanites; and the list goes on.

Christ taught throughout his ministry that sacrifice was absolutely necessary in order to inherit the Kingdom of God. Because of this stringent requirement, those He taught were counseled to count the cost before they became a disciple.

> *For which of you, intending to build a tower, sitteth not down first, and counteth the cost, whether he have sufficient to finish it? Lest haply, after he hath laid the foundation, and is not able to finish it, all that behold it begin to mock him, Saying, This man began to build, and was not able to finish. Or what king, going to make war against another king, sitteth not down first, and consulteth whether he be able with ten thousand to meet him that cometh against him with twenty thousand? Or else, while the other is yet a great way off, he sendeth an ambassage, and desireth conditions of peace. So likewise, whosoever he be of you that forsaketh not all that he hath, he cannot be my disciple. (Luke 14:28–33)*

At some point in our life, we will be required to give back to the Lord our most precious possessions. It may be going on a full-time mission; it may be rejecting friends and family in order to uphold a gospel principle; it may be dealing with the death of a loved one; or it may be accepting a very difficult calling. Whatever it is, it will come when we are ready and is a necessary step for our entrance into the Kingdom of God.

It was for the purpose of fulfilling this eternal principle for every member of the Church that the Law of Consecration and the United Order was established in these last days. Those who entered into the United Order were required to give all of their worldly possessions to the church for the building up of the Kingdom of God on earth. By doing so they became like Abraham, proving before God, angels, and the world that they put God and His Kingdom first in their lives. In return, they were sealed to eternal life by the Prophet of God.

By accepting and living the law of consecration, we obtain the faith necessary to enter the Kingdom of God. The time will come when you will be asked to sacrifice your Isaac, to be a Job, to flee as

Lehi and Brigham Young, or even to die, as our forefathers have done before us. You must find the inward strength to do this, or you cannot expect to enter the highest Kingdom of God. It is not enough to believe you can do it; you must prove you can do it. The faith and knowledge created by your sacrifices will give you the spiritual power required to obtain your calling and election and is the key to entering the celestial worlds.

Chapter Seven
Hope

Understanding the doctrine of hope is important to everyone; after developing our faith, it is the next vital step a person must take in order to obtain the Kingdom of God. Hope is not a wish. We have all "wished upon a star" or wondered what we would do if we found a genie in a bottle and had three wishes. But wishes are very different than hope. Wishes are dreams or desires that we have no realistic way of obtaining. Hope consists of a desire we have based upon a real expectation and ability to obtain such in the future. As in the previous sections on faith, we will start discussing the doctrine of hope by bringing together information that leads to a new definition of hope.

Hope: desire accompanied by expectation of fulfillment. (Webster Dictionary)

> *As used in the revelations, hope is the desire of faithful people to gain eternal salvation in the kingdom of God hereafter. It is not a flimsy, ethereal desire, one without assurance that the desired consummation will be received, but a desire coupled with full expectation of receiving the coveted reward. (Bruce R. McConkie,* **Mormon Doctrine,** *p. 365)*

Here is an example. If your new car suddenly stopped working and you knew absolutely nothing about engines, you would have little or no hope of fixing the car. You would be found standing on the side of the road, with the hood up, wishing there was something you could do. In reality, you would probably be forced to wait for the tow truck. On the other hand, if that same car broke down and the driver was an expert mechanic, he would have real hope that he could fix the car with full expectation of actually doing it. The mechanic's *knowledge* provided him a different level of trust in his ability to understand and correct the problem. He would not have to stand idly by wishing for some miracle to occur; he could actively ensure the desired result came to pass. He could not *guarantee* the result (hope is not a guarantee), but, because of his knowledge, he could hope for and expect a positive result.

The same is true of the gospel of Jesus Christ and the desire Christians have of obtaining the Kingdom of God. A person who has never read the scriptures, who only goes to church on Christmas and Easter, and who does not pray except, perhaps, during times of extreme hardship, *cannot* develop or obtain any real hope of obtaining eternal life. He cannot expect to obtain the Kingdom of God because he has done little or nothing to prepare himself for that goal. He would be wishing upon a star.

On the other hand, consider the example of a righteous man who has not only read all of the scriptures but has made a lifelong study of these "textbooks;" who not only attends church every Sunday but has faithfully fulfilled a myriad of callings and responsibilities; and who not only has developed his faith but has gradually increased his knowledge of God by participating in and witnessing many miracles, gifts of the Spirit, and answers to prayer. Unlike the previous example, this man has true hope of obtaining the Kingdom of God. This man can *expect* to receive a fulfillment of his desires. His *knowledge* and *works* have made it possible to enter the Kingdom.

The hope the scriptures talk about is much more than a limited expectation of a reward, it is a realistic expectation based upon actual revelation from God.

> *And also remember that thou hast said that thou has prepared*
> *a house for man, yea, even among the mansions of thy Father,*
> *in which man might have a more excellent hope; wherefore*
> *man must hope, or he cannot receive an inheritance in the*
> *place which thou hast prepared. (Ether 12:32)*

This "more excellent hope" that a man must obtain in order to inherit the Kingdom of God is nothing more or less than obtaining his calling and election. Remember, in order to have real hope, a person must have *knowledge*. Through the law of sacrifice, he must *know* that the life he is living is acceptable to God. And in order to know for certain that his life is acceptable to God, the man must receive a revelation, a witness to his soul by the Holy Ghost that confirms this knowledge. Once he has obtained this witness, he has a basis upon which to expect to inherit the Kingdom of God. He is not yet *guaranteed* to obtain this goal, but he now has hope.

> *Wherefore, whoso believeth in God might with surety hope for*
> *a better world, yea, even a place at the right hand of God,*
> *which hope cometh of faith, maketh an anchor to the souls of*
> *men, which would make them sure and steadfast, always*
> *abounding in good works, being led to glorify God. (Ether*
> *12:4)*

What is this "anchor" that makes us steadfast enough to inherit the Kingdom of God? It cannot be something that moves or changes, but must be a principle or doctrine that will actually prepare men to obtain what they seek. The Prophet Joseph said it best while describing the kind of hope and knowledge a man would have after obtaining his calling and election.

> *Now for the secret and grand key. Though they might hear the*
> *voice of God and know that Jesus was the Son of God, this*
> *would be no evidence that their election and calling was made*

sure, that they had part with Christ, and were joint heir with him. They then would want that more sure word of prophecy, that they were sealed in the heavens and had the promise of eternal life in the kingdom of God. Then, having this promise sealed unto them, it was an anchor to the soul, sure and steadfast. Though the thunders might roll and lightnings flash, and earthquakes bellow, and war gather thick around, yet this hope and knowledge would support the soul in every hour of trial, trouble, and tribulation. Then knowledge through our Lord and Savior Jesus Christ is the grand key that unlocks the glories and mysteries of the kingdom of heaven. (TPJS, p. 298)

CONCLUSION

Hope is a dynamic and specific step in our eternal progression. Having developed faith in Jesus Christ and the gospel He taught, we have the tools to obtain a sure knowledge about God. As we add the works of righteousness to our faith, we will experience many miracles: actual, physical manifestations of God in the real world. These precious and sacred experiences will give us perfect knowledge and will motivate us to become true servants of God. Our faith will grow until we are able to experience and endure the culmination of the law of sacrifice, our own personal and ultimate test. Then, as we continue to repent of our sins and make course corrections in our lives, the time will come (usually after many years) when our hearts and lives meet the requirements for entry into the Kingdom of God. We will be able to know when this happens because we will be able to look back upon the life we have led, compare it with what we have learned about the Kingdom, and realize that we are doing everything the Lord has asked of us. Then, if we ask, the Lord will witness to our souls whether or not our observation is true. If we receive this assurance, we will receive the hope the scriptures speak of and will finally find the peace about which Christ spoke.

> *Elder Ballard further said: "As we put our faith and trust to work, hope is born. Hope grows out of faith and gives meaning and purpose to all that we do. It can even give us the peaceful*

assurance we need to live happily in a world that is ripe with iniquity, calamity and injustice . . ." (Church News, *October 10, 1992, p. 9)*

This true peace of Jesus Christ comes from knowing we have finally found the path to the kingdom. But do not suppose that by reaching this step the struggle is over! Obtaining this hope simply motivates us to further perfect our lives and to work even harder in the service of our Lord and Savior.

> *Thus true hope focuses us on the great realities – "things as they really are" – and frees us from unneeded anxiety, but not from the necessity of patient endurance. When we are down and discouraged, the hope of Christ can lift us up lest we remain vulnerable overlong. The brisk pace of Church service also helps us focus talent and time outwardly rather than being left alone for long with our moods. Duties knocking at one's door are like friends come to call, not always convenient but usually gladdening in their effect. Our hope rests upon a dependable expectation. Let others, if they choose, define theological hope as a mere wish or an awaiting. Hope includes, in fact, these more passive ingredients. But it is so much more than wishful musing. It stiffens, not slackens, the spine. It is anticipation that turns into day-by-day determination. It is an eager and an enthusiastic expectation based upon a dependable and justifiable object of hope, the triumph of the resurrection-generating Lord Jesus Christ. It is this hope, and this hope alone, that permits us to "endure well" to the end – knowing that the end is but a glorious beginning! It is this same hope that is such a vital and helping virtue when we must "continue the journey" notwithstanding our weaknesses.*
> *(Neal A. Maxwell,* Notwithstanding My Weakness, *p. 49)*

Now that we have hope, we become free of many of the anxieties of life. We become free to pursue even more altruistic feelings and actions. We can concentrate on the final virtue of the righteous: charity. This does not mean we have not felt or experienced the pure love of Christ before this time—certainly not. Faith, hope, and charity, though guideposts along our path to the kingdom, are not mutually exclusive. In fact, all three are so entwined that we will experience them all, to one degree or another, at every step along the path!

> *Thus gospel hope is a very focused and particularized hope that is based upon justified expectations. It is a virtue that is intertwined with faith and charity, which virtues are not to be understood either when they are torn apart from each other or apart from the Lord Jesus Christ, without whom they are all vague virtues. Doubt and despair go together, whereas faith and hope are constant companions.* (Neal A. Maxwell, Notwithstanding My Weakness, p. 42)

It is important to recognize the freedom that real, scriptural hope gives us. It is like the proverb that one must know how to swim before teaching others to do so. Once we have a witness that our lives are acceptable before God, we no longer need to focus *all* of our efforts on saving ourselves! We now can turn our efforts to serving others. Now that we have the peace of God within our own hearts, we can share that love and peace with others. We can begin to develop the virtue of charity as God defines it.

Chapter Eight
Charity: The Pure Love of Christ

As we progress along the path to eternal life, we will begin to develop charity. Charity is not an action but a state of being. It is the ability to think, feel, and act like Jesus Christ. In our development, many try to live by the motto: "What would Jesus do?". Charity is the literal fulfillment of this goal. Charity is a celestial law. Those who live in the Celestial Kingdom must have this characteristic and ability imbedded within their souls in order to function and work within celestial realms. Without it they would be a fish out of water, totally incapable of using and controlling the knowledge and power available to them.

Charity is a concept that all Christians *believe* they understand: Charity is love, or, more specifically, the "pure love of Christ." But when they are asked to explain: "What is the love of Christ?" or "What does 'the love of Christ' mean?" or, "What does the love of Christ do?" few are able to produce a further explanation. It is like trying to define a word by using the word— it gets us nowhere. We must go beneath the surface to discover the real meaning behind charity.

Our best and one of the only real explanations of what charity is comes from the Apostle Paul. His letter to the Corinthians is the one place in the scriptures that gives us true insight on this most important subject. In Chapter 12 of 1 Corinthians, Paul talks about the gifts of the Spirit which are brought about by the development of faith in an individual. Then in Chapter 13, Paul expands our vision; he shows us that the end of the progression of our faith and hope is charity. Charity is the highest and most pure doctrine of Christianity. In fact, the prophets have clearly said that without developing charity, men will not be able to inherit the Kingdom of God. Truly, these three concepts are connected: faith, hope, and charity. We move from one to the next until we are prepared to inherit the Celestial Kingdom of our God.

> *"And now I know that this love which thou hast had for the children of men is charity; wherefore, except men shall have charity they cannot inherit that place which thou hast prepared in the mansions of thy Father." (Ether 12:34)*

First, we will talk about what charity *is not:*

According to Paul, all these things will have an end:[1]

1. Any and *all* of the gifts of the Spirit.
2. Spiritual knowledge and/or the mysteries of God.
3. Faith, even if that faith is strong enough to move mountains.
4. Worldly charity, or giving of one's worldly goods to the poor.
5. The principle of personal sacrifice.

This list is quite astounding in scope. Just consider this:

1. If a person like Isaiah, who had the gifts of the Spirit and could prophesy and heal, yet did not have charity, he would not make it to the Kingdom of God.
2. If a person like Joseph Smith, who more than any other person save Jesus Christ had the mysteries of the Kingdom of God revealed to him, yet did not have charity, he would not make it to the kingdom.

---

[1] 1 Corinthians 13:1–3

82

3. If people like Moses and Ether, who had faith to move mountains and produce great miracles, yet did not have charity, they would not make it to the kingdom.

4. Consider the Apostles of Christ, who gave up all of their worldly goods to follow their Lord, and understand that if they did not have charity, they would be locked out of the kingdom.

5. Even the great Patriarch Abraham, the father of the faithful, who was willing to sacrifice his only son Isaac, if he did not have charity, he would be cast out of the kingdom.

As incredible as this seems, it is true. The path of faith, hope, and charity must be followed by everyone, no matter what their station in life or when they were born. The doctrine of charity must be profound!

Secondly, let us see what charity *is:*

Paul explains that the following characteristics of charity will supercede the gifts of the spirit and will endure forever:[2]

long-suffering	kindness
does not envy	no pride
is never indecent or unbecoming	is not selfish
is not easily provoked	thinks no evil
does not rejoice in injustice or unrighteousness	rejoices in the truth
bears all things	believes all things
hopes all things	endures to the end

Paul completes his thoughts by telling us that all other attributes and gifts will change or vanish away, but charity will never fail. Its virtues will continue with us, and, as a part of us, into eternity.

---

[2] 1 Corinthians 13:4–8

Once again, we are astonished by this list of attributes. This special Christ-like love we are to have will overwhelm all other attributes and gifts we may develop during this life. It incorporates all of the attributes of a true Christian lifestyle. But there is something different about this special love: it is different than the love that comes naturally to us as part of our relationships one with another.

> *This may be the clearest of all scriptural teachings on the importance of doing the right things for the right reasons.*
>
> *The Apostle Paul echoed this fundamental truth of Christianity in his great sermon on charity: "And though I bestow all my goods to feed the poor, and though I give my body to be burned, and have not charity, it profiteth me nothing" (1 Corinthians 13:3). Clearly, unless motivated by pure love, even the most generous gifts of earthly treasures "profiteth . . . nothing." As Paul would later counsel Timothy: "Now the end of the commandment is charity out of a pure heart, and of a good conscience, and of faith unfeigned" (1 Timothy 1:5).*
>
> *We know from these inspired words that even the most extreme acts of service fall short of the ultimate 'profit' unless they are motivated by the pure love of Christ. If our service is to be most efficacious, it must be unconcerned with self and heedless of personal advantage. It must be accomplished for the love of God and the love of his children. The Savior applied that principle in the Sermon on the Mount, wherein he commanded us to love our enemies, bless them that curse us, do good to them that hate us, and pray for them that despitefully use us and persecute us (see Matthew 5:44; 3 Nephi 12:44). He explained the purpose of that commandment as follows:*
>
> *For if ye love them which love you, what reward have ye? do not even the publicans the same?*
>
> *And if ye salute your brethren only, what do ye more than others? do not even the publicans so? (Matthew 5:46-7).*
>
> *This principle — that our service should be for the love of God and the love of fellow men rather than for personal advantage*

or any other lesser motive – is admittedly a high standard. The Savior must have seen it so, since he joined this commandment of selfless and complete love directly to the ideal of perfection. The very next verse of the Sermon on the Mount contains this great command: "Be ye therefore perfect, even as your Father which is in heaven is perfect" (Matthew 5:48; see also 3 Nephi 12:48). (Dallin H. Oaks, Pure in Heart, pp. 23, 47–48)

When we love those who love us—the basis for the love we commonly understand and that is a part of our earthly relationships with one another—we do not reach the level of love and understanding that both Christ and Paul regarded as essential for a person to have true charity. The "pure love of Christ" was much broader in scope and much more difficult to obtain. It is a high standard—the highest—because it is a celestial virtue.

Perhaps the best way to explain how the "love of Christ" differs from the love we know and understand is to give an object lesson.

Parable of the Givers

There is a beggar on the street as three strangers pass by. Each person is a good Christian who has the love of God in his heart and an honest desire to help others. However, each has a very different approach to helping this man in need. The important question for you to answer is: Which person had *real* charity?

1. Feeling love and compassion, the first person gives money to the beggar.

2. Having a desire to help, but believing the beggar would just spend the money on alcohol or drugs, the second person buys food to give to the beggar.

3. Believing that the beggar is reaping what he sowed, and at the same time believing it is better to teach someone to fish rather than give them a fish, the third person gives the beggar his

business card, with an offer of employment and a chance to change his life for the better.

I am sure that there are many other scenarios that we could list, but as you will discover, the answer would be the same. We have all been in this situation before. Someone comes to us asking for money or food and we are immediately faced with the question: how do we best serve those who need our help? The scriptures are very clear that we have a responsibility to help the poor.

> *And now, for the sake of retaining a remission of your sins from day to day, that ye may walk guiltless before God – I would that ye should impart of your substance to the poor, every man according to that which he hath, such as feeding the hungry, clothing the naked, visiting the sick and administering to their relief, both spiritually and temporally, according to their wants. (Mosiah 4:26)*

Knowing that, as Christians, we have a responsibility to help those less fortunate than we, the question remains, *how* do we help them? True charity is the solution.

Now, what was your answer? Which stranger had true charity?

The answer will surprise most of you: *none* of them had charity! Why? Because none of them *knew* whether or not they were actually helping the beggar! What if the first person's money was used for alcohol or drugs? What if in the second situation the person needed medical attention, not food? What if in the third situation the person needed immediate help and could not wait for a week or two to earn money? All of these actions by good-intentioned people could have hurt more than helped the beggar. However, if these people *knew* what the beggar had really needed they could have been certain that their help was beneficial.

Knowledge is the key to understanding the mystery behind the doctrine of charity.

What is charity?

The Apostle Paul gives us the key to the mystery:

> *For we know in part, and we prophesy in part. But when that which is perfect is come, then that which is in part shall be done away. When I was a child, I spake as a child, I understood as a child, I thought as a child: but when I became a man, I put away childish things. For now we see through a glass darkly; but then shall I know even as also I am known. (1 Corinthians 13:9–12)*

In order to understand and develop true charity, we must understand what God would do to help those in need:

- Now we know in part, when we become like God we will know all things.
- Now we are all children in our understanding; we must become like adults in our ability to see the *big* picture. In other words, we must be able to see the long-term results rather than focus on the short-term pain. We must be able to find a cure, not just treat the condition.
- Now we see through a dark veil; then we will see the *truth*, clearly and with no misunderstanding.
- Now we only understand a little; then we shall know Christ just as He knows us—face to face, man to man. Our knowledge will break through the veil and we will be able to see clearly how things really are and what people really need.

In order to have charity, you must know that what you are doing will help the person.

We believe Paul was telling us that the ability to develop charity not only overwhelms and obscures all other gifts and blessings, but that the key to obtaining charity is to understand as God understands, to see specific situations as God would see them, and to act for and in behalf of people in the way God would if He were here on earth. In truth, all Christians know this to be true. How many times have we heard or asked the question, "What would Jesus do?" In order to make this adage a reality, we would have to know what God knows. And the only way we can obtain that kind of knowledge is to receive *direct revelation.*

Since only God has this kind of knowledge (we see through a glass darkly), we can have true charity only by receiving revelation from God concerning the person we are trying to help! I know that at first this must seem like an astonishing statement and an impossibility for mortal men, but it is true! Charity is a celestial law and a virtue that *can* be developed by righteous people.

When you think about it, most Christians have already experienced the ability and blessing of charity. Have you ever been inspired to help someone without really knowing why, only to find out later that what you did or gave is exactly what the person being helped needed at the time? This inspiration was nothing more or less than revelation from God prompting you to help at the right time and in the right way. This is *true* charity.

Many will immediately wonder: "Does that mean we should not, or cannot do anything to help others until we receive a revelation from God!?" Of course not. That would be silly. We have been told that *anything* we do to help others will be accounted to us for righteousness.

> *And whosoever shall give to drink unto one of these little ones*
> *a cup of cold water only in the name of a disciple, verily I say*
> *unto you, he shall in no wise lose his reward. (Matthew 10:42)*

Even if we do not always feel the whisperings of the Spirit, that does not exclude us from the responsibility to help others. True charity, through revelation from heaven, is a *goal* that we work for, and often achieve, when we attempt to use the process correctly. Like all doctrines and principles of the gospel, the ability to have the celestial quality of charity will not come all at once, or without great effort. We must first understand and then practice the principle daily so that, over time, we will be able to develop charity as an intrinsic virtue of our eternal souls.

Let me give you an example that everyone should be able to relate to:

> It is stated in the Book of Mormon that "charity is the pure love of God." By this plain yet comprehensive definition, we learn that unless the love of God dwells in our hearts we have not charity. This love for the salvation of mankind induces the true servants of the Lord to travel to the ends of the earth, without the shadow or hope of earthly reward, to preach the gospel to the world. (Matthias F. Cowley, Cowley's Talks on Doctrine, p. 167)

One of the goals of all missionaries in the field is to receive inspiration and revelation concerning where they should go to find people to teach the gospel. Though they may not receive specific revelation every day or for every person they teach does not mean they should sit in their apartment and wait for it! On the contrary, they are required to go out every day and serve the Lord the best way they know how. However, their *goal* is to struggle and fast and pray and progress in order to be prepared to receive inspiration and revelation from God when it comes. And it *does* come! Slowly, strangely sometimes,[3] but it does come.

It is the same with all of us in our efforts to help those around us. We should be fasting and praying and preparing to receive the inspiration of God concerning those we are serving. As we faithfully strive to do this, we will *learn* how the process of revelation works in our lives, and be able to progress to the point where we often experience true charity.

How do we obtain charity?

Charity, the highest attribute we can obtain, and the final step in our development as children of God, can be obtained by following the

---

[3] Isaiah 55:8

counsel of the prophets and by living all of the laws and ordinances of the gospel faithfully until they become part of our lives. As with all principles and laws of the gospel of Jesus Christ, charity begins with small steps, as directed by the Savior and his servants on earth, and ends with our ability to receive revelation and direction directly from God.

Let us take, for example, the law of tithing. The law of tithing is a commandment that one must live as part of our progression from simple faith to the obtaining of perfect knowledge. As we faithfully pay a full tithe, we begin to witness the blessings that come from living the law of tithing: the "windows of heaven" open up our hearts and minds to a much greater and purer understanding of giving.[4] When we first begin paying tithing, we do so for selfish reasons: we want to become members of Christ's church and receive the blessings promised us. But over time, and as our faith and understanding of celestial principles grow, our motives—the reasons *why* we give—change.

> The eternal significance of action or inaction turns on the state of mind that motivated the act or omission. Acts that seem to be good bring blessings only when they are done with a good motive, with real and righteous intent. We can work to reform our motives if we are continually asking ourselves: Why am I taking this action? That question is especially important for actions we suppose to be good. It reminds us that it is not enough to act in ways that seem to be good. We must act for the right reasons. If we truly desire to please God and serve him, continual self-examination of our reasons for actions cannot fail to expose our selfish and sordid motives and challenge us to reform them. The ultimate good motive for any act is charity– the pure love of Christ. We acquire that motive in two ways: 1) by praying for love, and 2) by practicing service. By praying for charity and by practicing service, we can reform our motives and come to be filled with the pure love of Christ that is characteristic of the pure in heart. (Dallin H. Oaks, Pure in Heart, p. 148)

---

[4] Malachi 3:8–12

As we move from simply keeping the commandments (paying tithing, etc.) to more altruistic actions, such as giving money to fast offerings and missionary work. God himself will begin to bless us with a greater love for those whom we are serving. In addition, as we actually begin to serve our fellow man by accepting and magnifying our church callings and assignments, our love for men in general will grow. We begin to develop charity by moving step by step in our actions and motivations until we develop a pure love, so that our actions are motivated by our desire to honor God and bless our fellow man. We move from selfish motivations, and being required to do things, to *wanting* to do things for others. We move from the telestial laws of keeping the commandments in order to receive blessings to the celestial laws of love and consecration.

> *When we reach the state of having "pure love of Christ" our desire to serve one another will have grown to the point where we will be living fully the law of consecration. Living the law of consecration exalts the poor and humbles the rich. In the process, both are sanctified. It would be a simple thing for the Lord to reveal to President Kimball where the deposits of oil and precious ores are. We could then hire someone to dig them out and we would float in wealth, and we would float right down to Hades. Only by voluntarily giving, out of an abundant love for his neighbor, can one develop that charity characterized by Mormon as the "pure love of Christ."*

> *(President Romney) said that to overcome giving grudgingly, members should live the commandments, give of themselves, care for their families, serve in Church callings, perform missionary work, pay tithes and offerings and study the scriptures, etc.*

> *As you lose yourself in this service, the Lord will touch and soften your heart and gradually bring you to the feeling with which He blessed the people in King Benjamin's time "that we have no more disposition to do evil, but to do good continually." As we individually become filled with the "pure love of Christ," we collectively evolve into a Church that is "pure in heart." It is not an impossible dream or an idealistic goal. We*

> *know this because the Lord has commanded us to become such.*
> *The final thing we are all to do is to consecrate all that we have*
> *to the building up of the kingdom of God, which includes car-*
> *ing for our fellow men. Doing this, we will hasten the advent*
> *of the millennium.* (Church News, October 10, 1981, p. 20)

One of the keys to finally moving into the realm of real charity is to understand that true charity involves the love of God and all mankind—even for those who don't deserve it. In order to move from a telestial love, or a love that is always rewarded, to a celestial love, a person must love and be willing to help those who sin and do evil. This is very difficult. But what celestial law is not difficult to live?

> *But does not love for God separate us from those who love Him*
> *not? The Prophet replies, writing from a damp, submerged*
> *dungeon, that God-like love, the unique love of those who walk*
> *uprightly, is without prejudice. And said he, "It gives scope to*
> *the mind which enables us to conduct ourselves with a greater*
> *liberality toward all that are not of our faith than what they*
> *have for themselves." (Teachings, p. 147) He taught, in fact,*
> *that it is a mark of our unfamiliarity with the principles of*
> *godliness when our affectionate feelings are "contrac-*
> *ted." (Teachings, p. 240) The closer we come to our Heavenly*
> *Father, he told some huffy sisters in Relief Society, the more we*
> *look upon perishing souls with compassion. "We feel that we*
> *want to take them upon our shoulders and cast their sins be-*
> *hind our backs." (Ibid) We love because of their partial or po-*
> *tential loveablility, not in spite of its absence. It follows, and he*
> *gave it as a lasting "key, that we know something in us has*
> *passed from life to death when we hate the breth-*
> *ren." (Teachings, p. 156–157, 197) Any brethren.* (Truman
> G. Madsen, Joseph Smith Memorial, p. 6)

In the end, true charity can be stated in the same simple terms as the two great commandments: love God with all of our hearts, and love our fellow men.

> *"Now abideth faith, hope, charity, these three; but the greatest*
> *of these is charity." Thus writes the Apostle Paul to the Corin-*
> *thian saints. Then what is charity? The Savior tells us that all*

92

the law and the prophets hang on these two commandments: "Thou shalt love the Lord thy God with all thy heart, with all thy soul and with all thy mind," and "thou shalt love thy neighbor as thyself." This then is charity, which is the fulfilment of the law. This is the greatest thing of all. This achieved will sanctify us from all unrighteousness and prepare us for celestial glory. (Rulan S. Wells, Conference Report, October 1929, p. 33)

Understanding charity at a higher level

The ability to have charity is directly related to obtaining our calling and election. As we grow in faith, obtain hope, and develop charity, we are taking the same steps that lead us to obtain our calling and election made sure. See how well these doctrines fit together:

Faith	Called	All who have *faith* are "called" or invited to enter the kingdom.
Hope	Elected	Those who prove themselves faithful are "elected" to enter the kingdom and obtain a real *hope* of attaining it.
Charity	Made Sure	When the righteous learn to have true *charity* in the service of others, they will have their election "made sure" or sealed.

Until we have perfect love we are liable to fall and when we have a testimony that our names are sealed in the Lamb's book of life we have perfect love, and then it is impossible for false Christs to deceive us. (TPJS, p. 9)

Contend earnestly for the like precious faith with the Apostle Peter, "and add to your faith virtue," knowledge, temperance, patience, godliness, brotherly kindness, charity; "for if these things be in you, and abound, they make you that ye shall neither be barren nor unfruitful in the knowledge of our Lord Jesus Christ." Another point, after having all these qualifications, he lays this injunction upon the people "to make your calling and election sure." He is emphatic upon this subject–

> *after adding all this virtue, knowledge, etc., "Make your call-*
> *ing and election sure." (TPJS, p 305)*

To be able to clearly see these two lines of connecting principles (faith, hope, and charity connected to calling and election made sure) will bring insight and instruction to both. Faith, hope and charity are a set of principles and characteristics that instruct us on what we must do—what kind of people we must become—in order to have our calling and election made sure and inherit the Kingdom of God. Our ability to understand what it is to have our calling and election made sure will give us an indication of where we are in our progress towards that goal and what we have yet to do to obtain it.

Understanding charity at an even *higher* level

> *Real charity is not something you give away. It is something*
> *that you acquire and make a part of yourself. (Elder Marvin J.*
> *Ashton, Church News, April 11, 1992, p. 2)*

Charity, the crown of the righteous, is the final step in our prepa-ration for the Kingdom of God. A righteous person who has charity will experience the following as he helps the needy:

1. You keep the commandments, so the Holy Ghost is your con-stant companion.
2. You pray often for others, so the Spirit of God can tell you who and how to help those in need.
3. Because you are guided by the Spirit, what you do will always help, even though you may not see the results immediately.
4. Even though you may not have the means or methods to ac-complish your task, you know that you can draw from an end-less supply (God owns everything) and with faith you move ahead.
5. No matter what you may end up sacrificing personally to ac-complish your task, God always finds ways to replenish and add to whatever you have lost.

Charity, the pure love of Christ, is a circle:

As we serve and give away our time, talents, money, possessions, etc., our resources are constantly replenished and expanded by God so we can carry the work further.

The key is to understand that when we are doing the will of God there is an eternal supply to draw upon. We only need to go and do the things which the Lord hath commanded, *knowing* that the Lord will provide the means and the way to accomplish our task.[5]

Charity *is* the pure love of Christ!

Charity is *not* just a representation of God's love, but it is His actual love—through revelation! We are not doing our will; we are carrying out His wishes for others. Just as men's use of the priesthood is not their own power or love—it is God's—charity is not *from* us, it is *through* us.

Let me give you an example. If we worked at a store and someone came to buy something, they would give us money and we would give them their purchase. Was the money ours? No. Was the item purchased ours? No. We were nothing more than employees. Both money and purchases passed through our hands without our benefiting at all (except for the pay we might receive from our employer). This is no different than the concept of charity. We work for God; we are his servants. People come to us for gifts and blessings, and, after consulting our Master, we give them the things they need. Their wants, needs, and desires pass through us to God, and what they receive in return is passed back through us from God. We do not receive any direct benefit from this transaction except for the "pay" we receive from God in the eternities, which is substantial: immortality and eternal life and all things the Father has available for our use. The concept is the same.

---

[5] 1 Nephi 3:7

This is also why God *must* replace what we have been asked to give: because *He* required it of us for *His* purposes. This is *not* a "sacrifice" as we understand the term; it is God's act of love through us to another person. That is why Paul can say that even though we sacrifice everything, even our own lives if necessary, it is not charity. We are *required* to perform acts of sacrifice in order to develop our faith and gain eternal hope. Sacrifice directly effects our ability to enter the Celestial Kingdom. Charity, however, is not a sacrifice. It is a gift from God that is given to the children of men through his servants. In our progression into the Kingdom of God, we must develop the ability to have charity, or in other words, we must become true servants of God by being able to let God work *through* us to serve others in the way God directs.

Why is it necessary for us to learn this principle? Because as we learn to do the Father's will in helping those in need, we will be able to help our own posterity, our spirit children, in eternity. Our charity now is for our brothers and sisters. Our charity then will be for our own children.

> *My charity is that God has provided for his children, the sons and daughters of Adam and Eve, where all who have lived according to the best light they had will have better kingdoms than ever entered into their hearts to conceive. That is the charity of God in his plans to save his people. He has designed that we should become Gods — the sons of God — fathers of eternal lives, like Abraham. (Brigham Young, Journal of Discourses, Vol. 8, p. 179)*

In the eternal worlds, when we have become equal partners with God and Christ[6] and have access to all that God has,[7] what will we do? There will be no such thing as greed because we will have everything we desire at our fingertips. Our work, the thing that will occupy our time (we must have something to do or eternal life will become incredibly boring), will be serving others—specifically, serving our own

---

[6] D&C 76:95; 88:107
[7] D&C 84:38

posterity. Our work and glory will be the same as our Father's—to bring to pass the immortality and eternal life of our spirit children.[8] In order to do this work, in order to give as God gives, we must understand the process of charity and be able to accomplish it. Since this world is but a training ground for eternity, it is in this life that we must learn the celestial principle of being able to give by letting the gifts pass through us to others rather than taking a part of it for ourselves. As we learn that the gift is not ours—we are just the messenger—God will be willing to pour more and more of his blessings through us to others. We become true servants, conduits of God to his children, and prepare ourselves to live in celestial realms.

It is vitally important to understand how this process works and have the faith to make it work. When we are inspired by God to help others and find obstacles in our way—be it time, money, ability, etc.—we must have the faith to understand that God will provide. This is not our gift or blessing; it is God's. And if we lack something in order to fulfill God's request, God is *obligated* to provide the talent, means, or time necessary for us to accomplish our task. We must bring forth the faith to understand that God *will* provide! And we must understand that God will replace anything of our own we might lose in the transaction, because it is God's duty and responsibility to make His servants whole. Since we are not dealing with the law of sacrifice, but God's personal gift to His children, God is responsible to pay for whatever he gives away at the hands of his servants. By understanding this principle, we will be able to develop the faith to do the works of God—because we will *know* that God will make us whole. So when the Spirit of God tells us to do something beyond that which we think ourselves capable, we will go forward with faith because we *know* that God must make the thing come to pass, because he is responsible to make good on his own requests.

---

[8] Moses 1:39

CONCLUSION

Charity is a celestial doctrine and an attribute that can only be understood when placed in its proper place among the other doctrines of faith and hope. Charity is the consummation of a righteous life, the crown that rests upon the head of the children of God who have developed the attributes of their Father. These are they who have faith to move mountains and create worlds, who have grasped the knowledge to control and govern the universe, and who have instilled within them the wisdom and love to use their power and knowledge wisely and with compassion. Before any person is given the ability to become equal with his God and Christ, he must *prove* that he can and will use the knowledge and power he holds in his hands with a pure love towards those he will serve and lead. Only then will the final veils of heaven be lifted and the final keys be given into his hand, which will close the final circle of knowledge. Alpha to Omega, the beginning to the end.

It is important to remember that in spite of our great spiritual progress, and no matter how much effort we spend in our service to God, we cannot be perfect while in this mortal existence. There was only one perfect being to inhabit this earth: Jesus Christ. Our goal, our responsibility, is to develop the qualities of righteousness within us. And as long as we have even a portion of the celestial attributes required to enter into the Kingdom of God, we will be permitted to enter. We cannot stress this point enough. We do not have to have faith enough to move mountains; we just have to have faith. We do not have to have knowledge enough to burst the veil of heaven; we must simply have a testimony that the life we are leading is a good one. And we do not have to save everyone who is in need or have revelation poured down upon us like Isaiah or Joseph; we simply need to understand the process of true charity and have experienced it in our lives. We must have a *portion* of these celestial virtues within us in order to make it into the Kingdom of God.

Ye who are quickened by a portion of the celestial glory shall then receive of the same, even a fullness. (D&C 88:29)

98

As with the doctrines of faith and hope, the seeds of charity must be planted, watered, and grown with care. And as with all things we receive from God, charity is a gift that can be developed until it bears fruit or it can be permitted to die. The former gives to us the ability to live a celestial life among the Gods. The latter brings eternal damnation; our progression as children of God into "adults" is stopped short and we are left to enjoy whatever station in life we have merited.

The choice is ours as it always has been and always will be. God will never force his children to become like him—that is Satan's way. But since we are children of God, we have placed within us the attributes and potential of our Father. And as we learned from the eternal law of attraction,[9] if we will but listen to the spirit of Christ that is within all of us,[10] we will be led step by step until we become exactly like our Father.

> *There is faith in man; just as there is hope and charity in every human being. No man, however savage or ignorant, has ever been discovered without these divine attributes. We have inherited all of these divine attributes because we are the children of God in very deed, and so man is made in the image of God both in spirit and in body, in physical form and in all of his faculties; the difference being that in the one they exist in their perfection, in the other in very imperfect form. And, there is meaning in the commandment of the Savior when he said: "Be ye therefore perfect, even as your Father in heaven is perfect."*

> *If we ever attain to those divine perfections, it will be because we have made the practical application of those principles that have within them the power of God unto our salvation. Every one of these attributes is susceptible of being developed and made perfect through the application of the principles of the Gospel, the most blessed thing, the greatest boon, the very pearl of great price that has been committed to men for the express purpose of perfecting their lives and preparing them for*

---

[9] D&C 88:40
[10] D&C 88:7–11

celestial glory. To accomplish this divine purpose God made this earth and placed us here upon it.

The love of Christ is the perfect thing that will supercede everything else. Then cultivate these Christian attributes, these divine attributes. They are ours to develop, the are in us, a part of our nature. (Rulon S. Wells, Conference Report, *October 1936, p. 89)*

In every aspect of our progression from simple intelligences to eternal beings, there is one most important ingredient: an act of will. From the beginning we have been given agency, or the ability to act for ourselves. In fact, without this ability, there would be no "existence" as we know it.[11] When you add to that agency the natural attributes and potential of God himself, there is nothing left for us to do but choose our destiny. If we choose to follow the spirit of Christ within us, we will seek the truth until we find it. Then, through an act of sheer will, we will *live* according to the truth we have found. By so doing, we will obtain an existence far beyond our wildest dreams. It is that simple and yet that profound. If we simply find the truth and live it, we will place the power of the universe within our hands, we will have the mysteries of eternity fill our minds with knowledge, and we will find our souls filled with a love of God. We will obtain perfect joy[12] and, in the end, we will have fulfilled the measure of our creation.

---

[11] D&C 93:30

[12] 2 Nephi 2:25

Chapter Nine
The Path to Eternal Life

The path to eternal life is strait and narrow and few find it. The Lord is a righteous and impartial judge. He does not and will not judge us subjectively as to which kingdom we inherit. God has provided a plan that has in it very specific events or actions in which a person must participate in order to qualify for the Kingdoms of God. If a person does not complete each of these open and visible steps to exaltation, they will not qualify!

An assurance that eternal life will be obtained in the world to come may be had in this world. As a matter of fact, the blessings of the celestial kingdom are promised only to those who have such an assurance. The Prophet Joseph Smith taught that one so sealed would have within himself an assurance born of the spirit, that he would obtain eternal life in the world to come. He urgently and repeatedly admonished the Saints of his day to obtain such an assurance by making their calling and election sure. It is this assurance within a person which brings to him the peace in this world which will sustain him in every tribulation. I conceive the blessings of the gospel to be of such inestimable worth that the price of them must be very exacting, and if I correctly understand what the Lord has said on the subject, it is. The price, however, is within the reach of us all, because it is not to be paid in money nor in any of this world's goods but in righteous living. What is required is wholehearted devotion to the gospel and unreserved allegiance to the Church of Jesus Christ of Latter-day Saints. We must demonstrate to the Lord that we are willing to serve him under all circumstances. When we have done this, we shall receive a assurance that we shall have eternal life in the world to come. (Marion G. Romney, General Conference 1949)

THE CHURCH OF THE FIRSTBORN

Perhaps the best way to understand the specific steps to obtain entrance into the Celestial Kingdom is to fully understand the Church of the Firstborn and its relationship to the earthly church.

Those who gain exaltation in the celestial kingdom are those who are members of the Church of the Firstborn ... There will be many who are members of the Church of Jesus Christ of Latter-day Saints who shall never become members of the Church of the Firstborn. To become a member of the Church of the Firstborn, as I understand it, is to become one of the inner circle.

The Lord has made it possible for us to become members of the Church of the Firstborn, by receiving the blessings of the house of the Lord and overcoming all things. Thus we become heirs, "priests and kings, who have received of his fullness, and of his glory," who shall "dwell in the presence of God and his Christ forever and ever," with full exaltation. (Joseph Fielding Smith, Doctrines of Salvation, 2:41–42)

The Church of the Firstborn *is* the inner circle: those faithful members of the Church who are worthy to enter the highest degree of glory in the Celestial Kingdom. The steps a person must make to enter this heavenly "church" are very similar to the steps we took to enter this earthly church:

1. We were *taught* the principles of the Gospel.
2. We received a *testimony* of the truth.
3. We received an earthly *ordinance* of baptism that formally and unconditionally brought us into the Church.

4. We received a *gift*, the gift of the Holy Ghost.

Now let us review the specific steps that are required to become members of the Church of the Firstborn.

1. How we are *taught* celestial doctrine

Like entering this earthly church, the first major step one must take to enter the Church of the Firstborn is to be taught what is required of each of us to become members. But instead of taking the missionary discussions, we go to the temple of the Lord to be taught.

When we enter the temple of the Lord, we take upon ourselves sacred covenants and are taught the specific steps we must take in order to actually enter the Celestial Kingdom. The ordinances and covenants we take upon ourselves at this point in time are only a teaching tool, a schoolmaster, because they are *conditional*. We are permitted to go back again and again, as we both serve and relearn these heavenly principles. It is important to understand that these temple ordinances are *conditional*. In fact, in the introduction to the endowment ordinance we receive an explanation concerning the conditional nature of all temple ordinances, with a promise that if we are faithful the time would come that we would be called up and anointed kings and priests, queens and priestesses. In other words, if we are faithful in living up to the covenants we make in the temple, some time in the future we will receive the real, unconditional ordinance that permits entrance into the Church of the Firstborn, or the Celestial Kingdom.

The prophets have made it clear that simply going to the temple and receiving one's endowment does *not* qualify a person for entrance into the Celestial Kingdom. A person must do more. A person must *be* more to qualify for this great blessing.

MAKING OUR CALLING AND ELECTION SURE. Those who press forward in righteousness, living by every word of revealed truth, have power to make their calling and election

103

sure. They receive the more sure word of prophecy and know by revelation and the authority of the priesthood that they are sealed up unto eternal life. They are sealed up against all manner of sin and blasphemy except the blasphemy against the Holy Ghost and the shedding of innocent blood. But the mere fact of being married for time and eternity in the temple, standing alone, does not give them this guarantee. Blessings pronounced upon couples in connection with celestial marriage are conditioned upon the subsequent faithfulness of the participating parties. (Joseph Fielding Smith Jr., Doctrines of Salvation, *2:46)*

It should be clearly understood that these high blessings are not part of celestial marriage...

Making one's calling and election sure is in addition to celestial marriage and results from undeviating and perfect devotion to the cause of righteousness. Those married in the temple can never under any circumstances gain exaltation unless they keep the commandments of God and abide in the covenant of marriage which they have taken upon themselves. (Bruce R. McConkie, Mormon Doctrine, *p. 110)*

In addition to confirming the fact that the temple endowment is only the start of what is needed to enter the Church of the Firstborn, the prophets have also confirmed that knowledge is the key to our progression. They confirm our need to be *taught* how to obtain our election to the Celestial Kingdom.

After having all these qualifications, he (the Apostle Peter) lays this injunction upon the people "to make your calling and election sure." What is the secret — the starting point? How did he obtain all things? Through the knowledge of Him who hath called him.

1st key: Knowledge is the power of salvation. 2nd key: Make your calling and election sure. 3rd key: It is one thing to be on the mount and hear the excellent voice, etc., and another to hear the voice declare to you, You have a part and lot in that kingdom (more sure word).

*Then knowledge through our Lord and Savior Jesus Christ is
the grand key that unlocks the glories and mysteries of the
kingdom of heaven.* (Teachings of the Prophet Joseph
Smith, *pp. 305–306*)

As we serve the Lord by accepting and magnifying the responsibilities given us in the church, we prove by our actions that we are committed to living the gospel of Jesus Christ and the temple endowment. During this learning period we are tried and tested; both to strengthen us and to prepare us for an ultimate test. But there is a difference between "tests" and "trials."

Throughout our life we are presented with a series of trials. Trials are situations that occur that show us our weaknesses and strengthen our faith. They are events or situations that we have little or no control of or choice about. For example when the Prophet Joseph Smith was killed, that became a trial for the saints. They had little choice or influence as to whether Joseph was killed or not; all they could do was deal with the consequences and try to remain faithful. If you become ill or someone in your family is in an accident or dies, you have no control or choice in this event—it is simply one of the many trials that are a part of this earthly experience. We must simply deal with our trials to the best of our abilities. We have no choice but to endure them and try to grow from them.

When we are spiritually prepared, there will come a period of testing. A test is a situation that is presented before us where we have a *choice* as to the outcome. For example, Abraham was presented with the test to sacrifice his son Isaac. He had a choice as to whether to fulfill the will of God in the matter or not. He chose to prove his faith and fulfill the commandment of the Lord. We will also have our tests: events and situations that will arise where we must choose the right path. Based upon the choices we make, we will either progress towards our goal or continue to learn from our mistakes and weaknesses.

As we prove ourselves by making correct decisions, we will continue to progress and truly begin to live the covenants we made in the temple. And as we continue in this progression, we prepare ourselves to make all of the sacrifices necessary for us to receive our calling and election to the Kingdom of God and see the face of God and live.

2. How we gain a *testimony* of our worthiness

The second step a person must take to enter the Church of the Firstborn is to be elected by receiving a testimony of their personal worthiness. Are we living the kind of life that will permit us to enter the Celestial Kingdom? This knowledge is critical in order for us to progress further! Christ has said that there is one strait path to eternal life. One path out of thousands—even millions—of false paths that are presented to us in our lifetime. How can anyone really know that he is on the right path? There is only one way: it must be revealed to us by God.

Once a person has repented of his sins, has been faithful in keeping the commandments, and has proven himself by the sacrifices he has made, *he will receive a testimony or assurance that the life he is now living is acceptable to God*, and that if he continues to live as he is now living, he will make it to the Celestial Kingdom. In other words, he is *elected* to enter the highest degree of the Celestial Kingdom; he has obtained his calling and election.

> But in the most express and proper usage of terms, 'The elect of God comprise a very select group, an inner circle of faithful members of the Church . . . They are the portion of church members who are striving with all their hearts to keep the fullness of the gospel law in this life so that they can become inheritors of the fullness of gospel rewards in the life to come. (Bruce R. McConkie, Doctrinal New Testament Commentary, Vol. 3, p. 331)

As President Romney said in the quote referenced at the start of this chapter, when a person receives their calling and election, they receive an *assurance*, or a *testimony* that they will obtain eternal life. This personal testimony can only be obtained by the sacrifice of all things . . .in other words, an ultimate sacrifice, or a sacrifice like Abraham giving up his only son Isaac.

> *When a man has offered in sacrifice all that he has for the*
> *truth's sake, not even withholding his life, and believing before*
> *God that he has been called to make this sacrifice because he*
> *seeks to do His will, he does know, most assuredly, that God*
> *does and will accept his sacrifice and offering, and that he has*
> *not, nor will not seek His face in vain. Under these circum-*
> *stances, then, he can obtain the faith necessary for him to lay*
> *hold on eternal life. Those, then, who make the sacrifice, will*
> *have the* testimony *that their course is pleasing in the sight of*
> *God; and those who have this* testimony *will have faith to lay*
> *hold on eternal life. But those who do not make the sacrifice*
> *cannot enjoy this faith. (Joseph Smith,* Lectures on Faith,
> *lecture six) (emphasis added)*

A person receives their calling and election when they receive a testimony by the Holy Spirit of Promise (the Holy Ghost) that they will receive eternal life. This is but one more step in the journey. It does not mean that they are a member of the Church of the Firstborn yet. To actually become a member of this heavenly church, one must first have a priesthood ordinance performed by one having authority.

Obtaining your calling and election simply means that you have received a personal revelation or promise that you will become a member of the Church of the Firstborn at some future date. It is a spiritual *prophecy* of your future.

In addition, and as stated before, this does not mean a person gets to see or has seen Christ. The visitation of the Savior is independent of this event, and is a step much further along in our progression. Many people may see the Savior in vision and yet never receive their calling and election. Many other people will have their calling and election and yet not have the opportunity to see the Savior. And, as incredible as it may seem, it is possible that people have sacrificed and proved themselves worthy to receive their calling and election and yet do not know it because they have not asked the Lord, nor sought for confirmation of this great blessing.

Here is a test to see if you have your calling and election. In the temple recommend interview with your Bishop, you will be asked if you are worthy to go to the temple. In order to pass the interview, you must answer "yes." In a similar way, if you can answer "yes" to the question, "Are you worthy to enter the Celestial Kingdom and live with God?" then you already have the "testimony" that Joseph Smith referred to. But it must be a strong and affirmative "yes," one born of the Spirit of God.

3. Obtaining the *priesthood ordinance*

After being called and then elected, we must patiently wait to receive the more sure word of prophecy, an earthly, physical evidence of our spiritual testimony. The more sure word of prophecy is a priesthood ordinance. It is the earthly confirmation that comes through the proper priesthood lines of authority that we have, indeed, received our Calling and Election.

> They then would want that "more sure word of prophecy,"
> that they were sealed in the heavens and had the promise of
> eternal life in the kingdom of God. (HC 5:388)

> The more sure word of prophecy means a man's knowing that
> he is sealed up unto eternal life, by revelation and the spirit of
> prophecy, through the power of the Holy Priesthood.
> (D&C 131:5) (emphasis added)

The personal revelation or testimony we receive when we are elected to enter the Celestial Kingdom is a prophecy about our future. It is the Spirit testifying or prophesying that our lives are acceptable to God and we therefore will be able to enter the Celestial Kingdom. However, it is one thing to know on a spiritual level and another to *actually* become a member of the Church of the Firstborn through a priesthood ordinance. In this step in our progression, we receive a more sure evidence or proof of the testimony we received concerning our standing before God. Or, in other words, we have our calling and election made sure, or made *unconditional*.[1]

> *What is meant by having one's calling and election made sure? To have one's calling and election made sure is to be sealed up unto eternal life; it is to have the unconditional guarantee of exaltation in the highest heaven of the celestial world; it is to receive the assurance of godhood; it is, in effect, to have the day of judgment advanced, so that an inheritance of all the glory and honor of the Father's kingdom is assured prior to the day when the faithful actually enter into the divine presence to sit with Christ in his throne, even as he is "set down" with his "Father in his throne." (Rev. 3:21) (Bruce R. McConkie,* Doctrinal New Testament Commentary, *Vol. 3, p. 331)*

> *Then I would exhort you to go on and continue to call upon God until you make your calling and election sure for yourselves, by obtaining this more sure word of prophecy, and wait patiently for the promise until you obtain it, etc. (James R. Clark,* Messages of the First Presidency, *Vol. 1, p. 179)*

After patiently waiting, the time will come when we are called to the temple by the Prophet of God. There we will receive our "second endowment" or receive the temple endowment without conditions attached to the covenants we take. We will be formally sealed up to eternal life in the highest degree of the Celestial Kingdom by the Prophet of God. We will become officially and unconditionally members of the Church of the Firstborn.

Remember that even though we formally become members of the Church of the Firstborn, we are not yet perfect and we can still commit sin. We can even fall from this high place and lose our standing before God (just as a member of the earthly church can be excommunicated for grievous sins). The difference is the type and severity of the

---

[1] See Note 1

punishment we receive for our sins. If we sin after being sealed to eternal life, we will be punished directly for our sins.[2] If our sins reach the level of murder, we will become like Satan and those that followed him—fallen angels and gods who are cast into outer darkness.[3] But frankly, this is nothing to fear. The whole purpose for the amount of testing we have to go through before reaching this point is to make sure we are ready for entrance into the kingdom, although there are always exceptions to the general rule.

4. The Gift

As powerful as the experience of being sealed to eternal life by the Prophet of God must be, it *still* does not mean that we have seen the Savior. However, the ordinance of the more sure word of prophecy brings with it the gift of the Second Comforter. Just as after baptism we receive the promise of the First Comforter (the Holy Ghost), after being sealed up to eternal life in the temple of God and confirmed members of the Church of the Firstborn, we will receive the gift of the Second Comforter: Jesus Christ.

> *When the Lord has thoroughly proved him, and finds that the man is determined to serve Him at all hazards,* then *the man will find his calling and his election made sure, then it will be his privilege to receive the other Comforter. Now what is this other Comforter?* It is no more nor less than the Lord Jesus Christ Himself. *When any man obtains this last comforter, he will have the personage of Jesus Christ to attend him, or appear unto him from time to time, and even He will manifest the Father unto him, and they will take up their abode with him, and the Lord will teach him face to face, that he may have a perfect knowledge of the mysteries of the Kingdom of God.* (Joseph Smith, **The Lectures on Faith**) (*emphasis added*)

---

[2] D&C 132:26
[3] D&C 132:27

This is the promise we all seek to obtain: the ability to see the face of God and live. After officially entering the Church of the Firstborn through the sealing ordinance in the temple, we will finally have the privilege to commune with God face to face and have the mysteries of the celestial worlds revealed to us.

> *It is the privilege of all those who have made their calling and election sure to see God; to talk with him face to face; to commune with him on a personal basis from time to time. These are the ones upon whom the Lord sends the Second Comforter. Their inheritance of exaltation and eternal life is assured, and so it becomes with them here and now in this life as it will be with all exalted beings in the life to come. They become the friends of God and converse with him on a friendly basis as one man speaks to another.*
>
> *After the true saints receive and enjoy the gift of the Holy Ghost; after they know how to attune themselves to the voice of the Spirit; after they mature spiritually so that they see visions, work miracles, and entertain angels; after they make their calling and election sure and prove themselves worthy of every trust – after all this and more – it becomes their right and privilege to see the Lord and commune with him face to face. Revelations, visions, angelic visitations, the rending of the heavens, and appearances among men of the Lord himself – all these things are for all of the faithful. They are not reserved for apostles and prophets only. God is no respecter of persons. They are not reserved for one age only, or for a select lineage or people. We are all our Father's children. All men are welcome. (Bruce R. McConkie,* The Promised Messiah, *p. 584)*

The person who has been sealed to eternal life will now have the opportunity to commune with the Savior from time to time, while he continues to progress. Yes, we still must progress. We are not yet perfect. As we continue to serve God in diligence and patience, the time will come when the Savior will even reveal to us the knowledge and presence of the Father.

Notes

1. Bruce R. McConkie, *Doctrinal New Testament Commentary*, 3:356.
    "The more sure word of prophecy means a man's knowing that he is sealed up unto eternal life, by revelation and the spirit of prophecy, through the power of the Holy Priesthood. (D&C 131:5) The annointing and sealing is to be called, elected and made sure."

Chapter Ten
The Witnesses

To close this book I thought it appropriate to give a glimpse of the experience that awaits those who have their calling and election made sure: the opportunity to see Jesus Christ and be in His presence. Though it is a reward that is beyond man's ability to express in mortal words, here are a few examples of some who have had this experience.

DESCRIPTIONS OF THE PREMORTAL JESUS CHRIST:

And they saw the God of Israel: and there was under his feet as it were a paved work of a sapphire stone, and as it were the body of heaven in his clearness. (Exodus 24:10)

And above the firmament that was over their heads was the likeness of a throne, as the appearance of a sapphire stone: and upon the likeness of the throne was the likeness as the appearance of a man above upon it. And I saw as the colour of amber, as the appearance of fire round about within it, from the appearance of his loins even upward, and from the appearance of his loins even downward, I saw as it were the appearance of fire, and it had brightness round about. As the appearance of the bow that is in the cloud in the day of rain, so was the appearance of the brightness round about. This was the appearance of the likeness of the glory of the LORD. And when I saw

it, I fell upon my face, and I heard a voice of one that spake.
(Ezekiel 1:26-28)

And the veil was taken from off the eyes of the brother of Jared,
and he saw the finger of the Lord; and it was as the finger of a
man, like unto flesh and blood; and the brother of Jared fell
down before the Lord, for he was struck with fear. And the
Lord saw that the brother of Jared had fallen to the earth; and
the Lord said unto him: Arise, why hast thou fallen? And he
saith unto the Lord: I saw the finger of the Lord, and I feared
lest he should smite me; for I knew not that the Lord had flesh
and blood. And the Lord said unto him: Because of thy faith
thou hast seen that I shall take upon me flesh and blood; and
never has man come before me with such exceeding faith as
thou hast; for were it not so ye could not have seen my finger.
Sawest thou more than this? And he answered: Nay; Lord,
show thyself unto me. And the Lord said unto him: Believest
thou the words which I shall speak? And he answered: Yea,
Lord, I know that thou speakest the truth, for thou art a God of
truth, and canst not lie. And when he had said these words,
behold, the Lord showed himself unto him, and said: Because
thou knowest these things ye are redeemed from the fall; there-
fore ye are brought back into my presence; therefore I show
myself unto you. Behold, I am he who was prepared from the
foundation of the world to redeem my people. Behold, I am Je-
sus Christ. I am the Father and the Son. In me shall all man-
kind have life, and that eternally, even they who shall believe
on my name; and they shall become my sons and my daugh-
ters. And never have I showed myself unto man whom I have
created, for never has man believed in me as thou hast. Seest
thou that ye are created after mine own image? Yea, even all
men were created in the beginning after mine own image. Be-
hold, this body, which ye now behold, is the body of my spirit;
and man have I created after the body of my spirit; and even as
I appear unto thee to be in the spirit will I appear unto my peo-
ple in the flesh. (Ether 3:6–16)

DESCRIPTIONS OF THE MORTAL JESUS CHRIST:

A description of Jesus Himself is found in *The Archko Volume* which contains official court documents from the days of the Messiah. In a chapter entitled "Gamaliel's Interview," it states concerning Jesus (Yhshua):

> *I asked him to describe this person to me, so that I might know him if I should meet him. He said: "If you ever meet him [Yhshua] you will know him. While he is nothing but a man, there is something about him that distinguishes him from every other man. He is the picture of his mother, only he has not her smooth, round face. His hair is a little more golden than hers, though it is as much from sunburn as anything else. He is tall, and his shoulders are a little drooped; his visage is thin and of a swarthy complexion, though this is from exposure. His eyes are large and a soft blue, and rather dull and heavy . . . ." This Jew [Judahite] is convinced that he is the Messiah of the world . . . this was the same person that was born of the virgin in Bethlehem some twenty-six years before . . . . (The Archko Volume, translated by Drs. McIntosh and Twyman of the Antiquarian Lodge, Genoa, Italy, from manuscripts in Constantinople and the records of the Senatorial Docket taken from the Vatican of Rome (1896) pp. 92–93)*

This is a reprinting of a letter from Pontius Pilate to Tiberius Caesar describing the physical appearance of Jesus. Copies are in the Congressional Library in Washington, D.C.:

TO TIBERIUS CAESAR:

> *A young man appeared in Galilee preaching with humble unction, a new law in the Name of the God that had sent Him. At first I was apprehensive that His design was to stir up the people against the Romans, but my fears were soon dispelled. Jesus of Nazareth spoke rather as a friend of the Romans than of the Jews. One day I observed in the midst of a group of people a*

young man who was leaning against a tree, calmly addressing the multitude. I was told it was Jesus. This I could easily have suspected so great was the difference between Him and those who were listening to Him. His golden colored hair and beard gave to his appearance a celestial aspect. He appeared to be about 30 years of age. Never have I seen a sweeter or more serene countenance. What a contrast between Him and His bearers with their black beards and tawny complexions! Unwilling to interrupt Him by my presence, I continued my walk but signified to my secretary to join the group and listen. Later, my secretary reported that never had he seen in the works of all the philosophers anything that compared to the teachings of Jesus. He told me that Jesus was neither seditious nor rebellious, so we extended to Him our protection. He was at liberty to act, to speak, to assemble and to address the people. This unlimited freedom provoked the Jews — not the poor but the rich and powerful.

Later, I wrote to Jesus requesting an interview with Him at the Praetorium. He came. When the Nazarene made His appearance I was having my morning walk and as I faced Him my feet seemed fastened with an iron hand to the marble pavement and I trembled in every limb as a guilty culprit, though he was calm. For some time I stood admiring this extraordinary Man. There was nothing in Him that was repelling, nor in His character, yet I felt awed in His presence. I told Him that there was a magnetic simplicity about Him and His personality that elevated Him far above the philosophers and teachers of His day.

Now, Noble Sovereign, these are the facts concerning Jesus of Nazareth and I have taken the time to write you in detail concerning these matters. I say that such a man who could convert water into wine, change death into life, disease into health; calm the stormy seas, is not guilty of any criminal offense and as others have said, we must agree — truly this is the Son of God!

Your most obedient servant, Pontius Pilate

The following description of Jesus Christ was written by Publius Lentrelus, a resident of Judea in the reign of Tiberius Caesar. It first appeared in the writings of Saint Anselm of Canterbury, 11th century:

There lives at this time in Judea a man of singular virtue whose name is Jesus Christ, whom the barbarians esteem as a prophet, but his followers love and adore him as the offspring of the immortal God. He calls back the dead from the graves and heals all sorts of diseases with a word or touch. He is a tall man, well-shaped, and of an amiable and reverend aspect; his hair of a color that can hardly be matched, falling into graceful curls, waving about and very agreeable crouching upon his shoulders, parted on the crown of the head, running as a stream to the front after fashion of the Nazarites. His forehead high, large and imposing; his cheeks without spot or wrinkle, beautiful with a lovely red; his nose and mouth formed with exquisite symmetry; his beard, and of a color suitable to his hair, reaching below his chin and parted in the middle like a fork; his eyes bright blue, clear and serene. Look innocent, dignified, manly and mature. In proportion of body most perfect, and captivating; his arms and hands delectable to behold. He rebukes with majesty, councils with mildness, His whole address whether in word or deed, being eloquent and grave. No man has seen him laugh, yet his manners are exceedingly pleasant, but he has wept frequently in the presence of men. He is temporate, modest and wise. A man for his extraordinary beauty and perfection, surpassing the children of men in every sense. (E. Raymond Capt's book, The Resurrection Tomb, *available from Artisan Sales, PO Box 1497, Thousand Oaks, California 91360)*

DESCRIPTIONS OF THE RESURRECTED JESUS CHRIST:

And as they thus spake, Jesus himself stood in the midst of them, and saith unto them, Peace be unto you. But they were terrified and affrighted, and supposed that they had seen a spirit. And he said unto them, Why are ye troubled? and why do thoughts arise in your hearts? Behold my hands and my feet, that it is I myself: handle me, and see; for a spirit hath not flesh and bones, as ye see me have. And when he had thus spoken, he shewed them his hands and his feet. And while they yet believed not for joy, and wondered, he said unto them, Have ye here any meat? And they gave him a piece of a broiled fish, and of an honeycomb. And he took it, and did eat before them. (Luke 24:36–43)

And I turned to see the voice that spake with me. And being turned, I saw seven golden candlesticks; and in the midst of the seven candlesticks one like unto the Son of man, clothed with a garment down to the foot, and girt about the paps with a golden girdle. His head and his hairs were white like wool, as white as snow; and his eyes were as a flame of fire; and his feet like unto fine brass, as if they burned in a furnace; and his voice as the sound of many waters. And he had in his right hand seven stars: and out of his mouth went a sharp two-edged sword: and his countenance was as the sun shineth in his strength. And when I saw him, I fell at his feet as dead. And he laid his right hand upon me, saying unto me, Fear not; I am the first and the last: I am he that liveth, and was dead; and, behold, I am alive for evermore, Amen; and have the keys of hell and of death. (Revelation 1:12–18)

And I saw heaven opened, and behold a white horse; and he that sat upon him was called Faithful and True, and in righteousness he doth judge and make war. His eyes were as a flame of fire, and on his head were many crowns; and he had a name written, that no man knew, but he himself. And he was clothed with a vesture dipped in blood: and his name is called The Word of God. And the armies which were in heaven followed him upon white horses, clothed in fine linen, white and clean. And out of his mouth goeth a sharp sword, that with it he should smite the nations: and he shall rule them with a rod of iron: and he treadeth the winepress of the fierceness and wrath of Almighty God. And he hath on his vesture and on his thigh a name written, KING OF KINGS, AND LORD OF LORDS. (Revelation 19:11–16)

And it came to pass, as they understood they cast their eyes up again towards heaven; and behold, they saw a Man descending out of heaven; and he was clothed in a white robe; and he came down and stood in the midst of them; and the eyes of the whole multitude were turned upon him, and they durst not open their mouths, even one to another, and wist not what it meant, for they thought it was an angel that had appeared unto them. And it came to pass that he stretched forth his hand and spake unto the people, saying: Behold, I am Jesus Christ, whom the prophets testified shall come into the world. And behold, I am the light and the life of the world; and I have drunk out of that bitter cup which the Father hath given me, and have glorified the Father in taking upon me the sins of the world, in the which I have suffered the will of the Father in all things from the beginning. And it came to pass that when Jesus had spoken these words the whole multitude fell to the earth; for they remembered that it had been prophesied among them that Christ should show himself unto them after his ascension into heaven. And it came to pass that the Lord spake unto them saying: Arise and come forth unto me, that ye may thrust your hands into my side, and also that ye may feel the prints of the nails in my hands and in my feet, that ye may know that I am the God of Israel, and the God of the whole earth, and have been slain for the sins of the world. And it came to pass that the multitude went forth, and thrust their hands into his side, and did feel the prints of the nails in his hands and in his feet; and this they did do, going forth one by one until they had all gone forth, and did see with their eyes and did feel with their hands, and did know of a surety and did bear record, that it was he, of whom it was written by the prophets, that should come. (3 Nephi 11:8–15)

LATTER-DAY DESCRIPTIONS OF JESUS CHRIST

Joseph Smith

"I saw a pillar of light exactly over my head, above the brightness of the sun, which descended gradually until it fell upon me. It no sooner appeared than I found myself delivered from the enemy which held me bound. When the light rested upon me I saw two Personages, whose brightness and glory defy all description, standing above me in the air. One of them spake unto me, calling me by name and said, pointing to the other—This is My Beloved Son. Hear Him!" (*Joseph Smith—History* 1:16–17)

Joseph Smith and Sidney Rigdon

"And while we meditated upon these things, the Lord touched the eyes of our understandings and they were opened, and the glory of the Lord shone round about. And we beheld the glory of the Son, on the right hand of the Father, and received of his fullness; and saw the holy angels, and them who are sanctified before his throne, worshiping God, and the Lamb, who worship him forever and ever. And now, after the many testimonies which have been given of him, this is the testimony, last of all, which we give of him: That he lives!" (D&C 76:19–22)

Joseph Smith and Oliver Cowdery

"We saw the Lord standing upon the breastwork of the pulpit, before us; and under his feet was a paved work of pure gold, in color like amber. His eyes were as a flame of fire; the hair of his head was white like the pure snow; his countenance shone above the brightness of the sun; and his voice was as the sound of the rushing of great waters, even the voice of Jehovah, saying: I am the first and the last; I am he who liveth, I am he who was slain; I am your advocate with the Father." (D&C:110:2–4)

George F. Richards

"The Lord has revealed to me, by dreams, something more than I have ever understood or felt before about the love for God and the Love for fellow men. More than forty years ago I had a dream, which I am sure was from the Lord. In this dream I was in the presence of my

Savior as he stood in midair. He spoke no word to me, but my love for him was such that I have not words to explain. I know that no mortal man can love the Lord as I experienced that love for the Savior unless God reveals it unto him. I would have remained in his presence, but there was a power drawing me away from him, and as a result of that dream I had this feeling that no matter what might be required at my hands, what the gospel might entail unto me, I would do what I should be asked to do, even to the laying down of my life." (*Conference Report*, October 1946, p. 139)

Clawson Journal

"After a long period of sincere repentance, my Bishop told me that I was clean of my sins and ready to become a priesthood holder. It was during this exciting time of rejuvenation that I had the most marvelous dream. My grandmother had taken me to see the film *The Three Witnesses* about the witnesses to the Book of Mormon. It had a tremendous impact upon me—actually 'seeing' angels appear to men on earth and realizing that it was really possible. I went home that night filled with awe and feeling the wonderful presence of the Spirit. That very night I had a dream, perhaps you would even call it a vision.

"I found myself inside a dark cave. The walls were moist and it was cold. You could tell that the cave was very deep, and I knew that I was totally lost. I was standing in front of a platform or podium of some kind, and on the platform was a book and a candle that was lit. I sensed that I had been reading in this book in the hope of finding a way out of the cave. I assume that the book was the *Book of Mormon* or perhaps one of the other scriptures. As I read, anxiously looking for the way out of the cave, I noticed a light coming from behind me. It was my brother, holding a candle in one hand and beckoning me with the other (my brother had been the one who persuaded me to come back to the Mormon Church). Suddenly the Holy Ghost fell upon me with great force, as I realized he knew the way out of the cave and that I would be free.

"As I felt the power of the Spirit of God within me, I suddenly saw before me a picture of the brother of Jared. I remembered reading how he had seen the finger of God, and that through his faith, he was able to break through the veil and see Jesus Christ for himself. Then, as strange as it may sound, I said to myself, if the brother of Jared could do it, I can do it. Upon simply thinking that one thought, the Spirit fell upon me again, this time even stronger than before, and I began to feel myself rise up in the air. The only way I can explain it, was that it was as if great weights were being lifted off my shoulders, which had been holding me down. As the weight was removed, my body felt so light and free, it began rising. The higher I climbed, the brighter it became, and the faster I rose. Soon I was rising at an incredible rate of speed, and then everything went completely white.

"The next thing I knew, I was sitting on a bed in a beautiful white room. It had a white tile floor, the walls and ceiling were white, even the clothes I was wearing were white. It quickly came to me that I had made it! I had made it into the Kingdom of God! The feelings of joy and happiness I had are truly beyond description. I remember looking at my hands and feeling the bedspread, just to make sure that I was really there. Everything was so real. I was forced to conclude that what I was experiencing was real. As I finally began coming to my other senses, I heard people talking and laughing outside my door. It was the most beautiful laughter you could imagine. There was such joy and happiness in their voices! The door to my room was slightly open, and I could see people walking past my door, all going in the same direction. As I opened my door all the way, I could see that it opened into a long hallway, filled with other doors like mine that also opened into it. To my right, the hallway seemed to go on forever, and I could not see the end of it. It was from that direction that all of the people who filled the hall were coming. As I followed their progress and turned to look to my left, I saw that the hall continued for some time to my left also. However, at the end of the long hall was a door that opened into a larger room. It was into this room that all of these other people were going. Not knowing what else to do, I turned to my left and began following the rest of the people towards the door at the end of the hall.

122

"Suddenly, a thought hit me with great force, and I immediately knew that there would be someone inside that door, greeting all those who were coming. I knew it would be my Savior, Jesus Christ! My excitement overcame me, and I began running down the hall towards the open door. As I burst through the door and into a large meeting room, I looked to my right and saw Jesus Christ standing there, greeting his guests. I ran to where he was standing and fell at his feet. At this point my emotions totally failed me, and I began weeping uncontrollably, bathing his feet with my tears, and holding onto his legs. After some time, I felt his hands on my arms, lifting me up to my feet. He told me that I no longer needed to kneel to him—that I had made it to the kingdom, and was therefore equal with him. I hesitated briefly but finally lifted my bowed head and looked at his face and into his eyes. As our eyes met, I felt a wonderful power of love and light begin to fill my body. There are no earthly words that can describe the intense, fulfilling experience that occurred as I felt my Lord and Savior's love towards me. Everything went white again, as the intensity of the experience overcame me.

"The next thing I remember was sitting at a long table. Jesus Christ was sitting at the head of the table, and I was sitting on his left (I knew that I was given this privilege only because I was a guest and not because of any right or position I held). I began asking Christ questions. I only remember two. I asked whether or not the great philosopher Confucius had also made it to his kingdom (this question arose because, prior to coming back into the Church, I had studied the Eastern religions and had been deeply affected by the wisdom and teachings of Confucius). Christ called down the table to someone and soon I was standing, shaking hands and conversing with Confucius. The next question I asked was whether or not we 'went on from here'—in other words, was this place and experience the end, or did we progress even further. Christ nodded yes, that we did continue to progress to even greater degrees of glory than the one I was there experiencing. Then everything went white again.

"I found myself wide awake and lying face up on the bed in my room, staring at the ceiling. I also found that I could not move. My body was still so full of the Spirit of God that it seemed to 'hum' or vibrate with energy. Very slowly the intense feelings died away, and I fell asleep.

"It has been said before, but I testify that it is true—that words cannot describe the wonderful experience that I had, and the powerful feelings of love and joy I felt in the presence of my Savior. I will do anything and everything within my power to find my way back into His presence again. Earthly feelings and material things have become base and ugly compared to what I saw and experienced in the Kingdom of God. I learned firsthand that there is nothing in this life, no amount of wealth, no honor or power, that can compare with what I received in just the brief time I was with my Savior. And though I consider myself one of the weakest of God's children, I know that I will do whatever I must to find myself back in that place again. I add my testimony to the long list of those who can and have testified before me: that He lives! That Christ is the Son of God, and that it is through his power and love that we are healed and made worthy to return and live with our Father again. I testify that these things are true! Amen." (from the Clawson Family Journal)

Melvin J. Ballard

"I recall an experience which I had two years ago, bearing witness to my soul of the reality of his death, of his crucifixion, and his resurrection, that I shall never forget. I bear it to you tonight, not with a spirit to glory over it, but with a grateful heart and with thanksgiving in my soul, that I know that he lives, and I know that through him men must find their salvation, and that we cannot ignore this blessed offering that he has given us as the means of our spiritual growth to prepare us to come to him and be justified . . . I found myself one evening in the dreams of the night in that sacred building, the temple. After a season of prayer and rejoicing I was informed that I should have the privilege of entering into one of those rooms, to meet a glorious Personage, and as I entered the door I saw, seated on a raised platform, the most glorious Being my eyes have ever beheld, or that I ever conceived existed in all the eternal worlds. As I approached to be introduced, he arose and stepped towards me with extended arms, and he smiled as he softly spoke my name. If I shall live to be a million years old, I shall never forget that smile. He took me into his arms and kissed me, pressed me to his bosom, and blessed me, until the marrow of my bones seemed to melt! When he had finished, I fell at his feet, and, as I bathed them with my tears and kisses, I saw the prints of the nails in the feet of the Redeemer of the world. The feeling that I had in the presence of him who hath all things in his hands, to have his love, his affection, and his blessing was such that if I ever can receive that of which I had but a foretaste, I would give all that I am, all that I ever hope to be, to feel what I then felt!" (*Improvement Era,* October 1919, 22:1028–32).

CONCLUSION

Everyone who hopes to return to live with our Father in Heaven must go through the same steps, make the same covenants, and similar sacrifices. No one is exempt. Even little children who die in infancy are not exempt. Even Jesus Christ was not exempt.

We may not all obtain our calling and election and have it made sure in this life; but whether in this life or in the next, we must all go through these same steps.

If we are willing to take the necessary steps, if we are willing to make the necessary sacrifices, we can and will obtain our calling and election and be sealed up unto eternal life. Then we, like our fathers before us, will be privileged to see the face of God and live.

Bibliography

Andrus, Hyrum. *Principles of Power.*
Ballard, Melvin J. General Conference Report, April, 1925.
Ballard, Melvin J. *Sermons of Melvin Ballard.*
Book of Jasher.
Capt. E. Raymond. *The Resurrection Tomb.*
The Church of Jesus Christ of Latter-day Saints. *Church News.*
The Church of Jesus Christ of Latter-day Saints. *Conference Reports.*
Clark, James R. *Messages of the First Presidency.*
Cowley, Matthias. *Cowley's Talks on Doctrine.*
Encyclopedia Americana, 1990.
Jessee, Dean. *The John Taylor Journal.*
The Journal of Discourses Volumes 1–26.
Kimball, Heber C., *The Life of Heber C. Kimball.*
Kimball, Spencer W. *The Teachings of Spencer W. Kimball.*
Letter from Pontius Pilate to Tiberius Caesar, Congressional Library, Washington, DC.
Madsen, Truman A. *Joseph Smith Memorial.*
Maxwell, Neal A. *Deposition of a Disciple.*
Maxwell, Neal A. *Not My Will, But Thine.*
Maxwell, Neal A. *Notwithstanding My Weakness.*
McConkie, Bruce R. *A New Witness for the Articles of Faith.*
McConkie, Bruce R. *Doctrinal New Testament Commentary.*
McConkie, Bruce R. *Mormon Doctrine.*
McConkie, Bruce R. *The Promised Messiah.*

McConkie, Bruce R. *The Mortal Messiah.*

McIntosh, Dr. and Dr. Twyman, Antiquarian Lodge. *The Archko Volume from manuscripts in Constantinople and the records of the Senatorial Docket, the Vatican of Rome.*

Oaks, Dallin H. *Pure in Heart.*

Richards, George F. *Conference Reports, October 1946.*

Romney, Marion G. *General Conference Talk, 1949.*

Smith, George Albert. *Sharing the Gospel with Others.*

Smith, Joseph, Jr. *History of the Church of Jesus Christ of Latter-day Saints.*

Smith, Joseph, Jr. *Lectures on Faith*

Smith, Joseph Fielding. *Church History and Modern Revelation.*

Smith, Joseph Fielding. *Doctrines of Salvation.*

Smith, Joseph Fielding. *Teachings of the Prophet Joseph Smith.*

Smith, Joseph Fielding. *The Restoration of All Things.*

The Standard Works: *The Book of Mormon: Another Testament of Jesus Christ, The Doctrine of Covenants, The Holy Bible, The Pearl of Great Price.*

Taylor, John. *The Gospel Kingdom.*

Tuchman, Barbara. *The Bible and the Sword.*

Velikovsky, Immanuel. *Worlds in Collision.*

Index